Acclaim for
The Complete Story of Sadako Sasaki

"My grandfather, Harry S. Truman, never spoke to me about the atomic bombings of Japan. Like most Americans, I learned about them in school. Textbooks didn't give me much more than casualty figures. Nothing about what really happened to the people on the ground. Sadako Sasaki's story was the first human story of the bombings I'd ever read. It led me to Masahiro and two visits to Hiroshima and Nagasaki, the second, with my son, Wesley, to record survivor testimony for the Truman Presidential Library. In all that time, Masahiro rarely told his own version of his family's story, preferring to focus on his sister's courage and selflessness. Now, we have the full story of the courage and selflessness of the entire Sasaki family, their friends and the people of Hiroshima."
Clifton Truman Daniel
Grandson of President Harry S. Truman

"Born in Hiroshima in 1943, Sadako Sasaki was two years old when she experienced the atomic bombing. She lived life as fully as she could, but it was cut short at the young age of twelve. The powerful message she proclaimed throughout her entire life still resonates with us all: Peace in our world can be achieved not through holding grudges but through striving to live our lives with compassion for others. Hope will be born from overcoming our differences, from profound understanding of one another, and from respect for our fellow human beings."
Kazumi Matsui
Mayor, Hiroshima, Japan

"When children make a crane it gives them a personal connection to a tragedy that they might otherwise not grasp because its horrific dimensions surpass normal imagination. Focusing on one person's story opens the possibility of becoming engaged in the abolition of nuclear weapons. If a mere one hundred explode every person's life on this frail planet will suffer beyond normal imagination and we must never let that happen."
Jonathan Granoff
President, Global Security Institute

"*The Complete Story of Sadako Sasaki* reminds us of our essential goodness and belongs in libraries, classrooms, and homes everywhere. Sadako inspires us to connect with others, recognize their needs, and act accordingly regardless of our personal circumstances. *Omoiyari-no-kokoro*, the act of showing empathy and concern, is demonstrated over and over again, as both Sadako and the authors offer us an opportunity to understand the joy of living beyond ourselves. The Peace Crane Project, described in the epilogue, is a beautiful opportunity to experience this joy and help create the conditions for a culture of peace."
Dr. Dorothy J. Maver
President, National Peace Academy

"This book tells the story of a young girl, Sadako Sasaki, an innocent victim of war. While in the hospital, twelve-year-old Sadako folded one thousand paper cranes in the hope of recovering from her atomic bomb-induced disease, and then she continued folding another one thousand paper cranes for her father. The book was written to inform young readers of Sadako's struggle and to inspire them to take action for peace. I believe it succeeds on both counts.

In Santa Barbara, the Nuclear Age Peace Foundation and La Casa de Maria created Sadako Peace Garden, a beautiful, natural garden in honor of Sadako, and each year we hold a commemoration in the garden on or about August 6 (Hiroshima Day), which we refer to as Sadako Peace Day."
Dr. David Krieger
President, Nuclear Age Peace Foundation

"Through reading the story of Sadako Sasaki you will know that the abolition of nuclear weapons and the rejection of war are the only path to survival for mankind. As you read the unbearable tragedy brought by the atomic bombing, you will learn the real meaning of 'to live' from Sadako, who patiently fought against an incurable disease that was so hard to endure. I hope you make many friends through the symbolic 'paper crane' left to us by Sadako. Please build a peaceful future together."
Dr. Tadatoshi Akiba
Former Mayor, Hiroshima, Japan

The Complete Story of
Sadako Sasaki
and the Thousand Cranes

Sue DiCicco *and*
Sadako's brother Masahiro Sasaki

TUTTLE Publishing
Tokyo | Rutland, Vermont | Singapore

Published by Tuttle Publishing, an imprint of Periplus Editions (HK) Ltd.

www.tuttlepublishing.com

Copyright © 2020 by Sue DiCicco and Masahiro Sasaki
Translation work by Naomi Nakagoshi and Anne Prescott

All rights reserved. No part of this publication may be reproduced or utilized in any form or by any means, electronic or mechanical, including photocopying, recording, or by any information storage and retrieval system, without prior written permission from the publisher.

LCCN 2022435820

ISBN 978-4-8053-1617-7

Distributed by

North America, Latin America & Europe
Tuttle Publishing
364 Innovation Drive
North Clarendon, VT 05759-9436 U.S.A.
Tel: 1 (802) 773-8930
Fax: 1 (802) 773-6993
info@tuttlepublishing.com
www.tuttlepublishing.com

Japan
Tuttle Publishing
Yaekari Building 3rd Floor
5-4-12 Osaki
Shinagawa-ku
Tokyo 141-0032
Tel: (81) 3 5437-0171
Fax: (81) 3 5437-0755
sales@tuttle.co.jp
www.tuttle.co.jp

Asia Pacific
Berkeley Books Pte. Ltd.
3 Kallang Sector #04-01
Singapore 349278
Tel: (65) 6741 2178
Fax: (65) 6741 2179
inquiries@periplus.com.sg
www.tuttlepublishing.com

29 28 27 26 25   10 9 8 7

Printed in Singapore   2411TP

TUTTLE PUBLISHING® is a registered trademark of Tuttle Publishing, a division of Periplus Editions (HK) Ltd.

Table of Contents

Preface ix

CHAPTER 1. A Most Unusual Arrival................ 3

CHAPTER 2. Life in the Midst of War 9

CHAPTER 3. Dark Days Looming 15

CHAPTER 4. The Unthinkable...........................19

CHAPTER 5. Hell on Earth.................................25

CHAPTER 6. Surrender and Hardship...............35

CHAPTER 7. The Bumpy Road to Recovery.....45

CHAPTER 8. Joys of Everyday Life 51

CHAPTER 9. A Different Kind of Pain 57

CHAPTER 10. Devastating News.......................63

CHAPTER 11. Holding on to Happiness 67

CHAPTER 12. Treatment Begins 73

CHAPTER 13. Graduation 77

CHAPTER 14. Hospital Life 81

CHAPTER 15. All Pain, No Gain.......................87

CHAPTER 16. Lost in the Stars 91

CHAPTER 17. Dreams Take Flight....................99

CHAPTER 18. Little Outings............................103

CHAPTER 19. A Secret Wish 115

CHAPTER 20. Pain-Free at Last 121

CHAPTER 21. Cranes Take Flight 127

Epilogue 135

Do you know that the wind feels good?

Do you know that the air is delicious?

To walk without worry.

To sleep without care.

To eat without concern.

So many take for granted these simple pleasures.

Do you? I hope you do not.

Be thankful for these things.

I want to tell you, they are wonderful.

—SADAKO SASAKI

Preface

Thoughts from Sue DiCicco

Sadako Sasaki was a young girl of twelve when leukemia, most likely caused by exposure to the atom bomb dropped on her city of Hiroshima, Japan, at the end of World War II, took her life.

Like many people in Japan, Sadako learned to fold origami cranes and believed that folding cranes might lead to the granting of a wish.

So much of what I read about Sadako was contradictory and felt incomplete. What did this brave young girl experience and how did her own family remember her?

My desire to learn more about Sadako's story propelled me to contact Masahiro Sasaki, Sadako's older brother. Masahiro-san became a gracious, supportive, informative, and generous partner in my quest, providing not only Sadako's story as he remembered it, but a broad and thoughtful perspective on war, life, and our collective power and responsibility to create a positive future for children everywhere.

This book is the result of our meeting and collaboration in telling Sadako's complete story.

Our translator, Naomi Nakagoshi worked beyond all expectation, to not only facilitate communication but research dates and facts, and connect me with other survivors and scholars in Japan. She was an integral part of the journey and invaluable in bringing Sadako's story to life.

Sadako's story is similar to the story of thousands of children of Hiroshima and Nagasaki. Many suffered and died at the time of the bombings and in the decades that followed. While it was Sadako who became an icon to many, and a symbol of the horrors of war, this book is dedicated to all those who suffered, and to those who keep the lessons of history in their minds and the dreams of a peaceful planet in their hearts.

Thoughts from Masahiro Sasaki

I believe Sadako was given a specific mission, a reason she was born into this world. My sister was a gifted child, borrowed from heaven. My family was entrusted with her care and the opportunity to have her with us for twelve short years. Her mission is why I think she was able to withstand anguish and pain that was beyond our imagination. She wrapped and concealed all the terrible conditions she received in her small heart.

Before her illness, she was such a happy child compared to other children. As cancer consumed her, she dropped from the culmination of that happiness to the bottom of misfortune. The reasons were many. Extreme poverty enveloped our family because of our father's promise to a neighbor. Sadako endured severe and constant pain caused by the cancer. She fell into extreme psychological distress, feeling she must keep her feelings and fear of death hidden from both her parents and me, and all her doctors, nurses, and friends.

Such conditions were far beyond the limits of the patience of most. But young Sadako, a twelve-year-old girl, endured such conditions for eight months. I believe Sadako was able to withstand such sufferings and trials because she was aware this was her mission. Her mission was to use her life, given from heaven to the utmost and to live for others. Sadako lived it and taught it.

The last words she left for us, even after enduring enormous suffering, were "thank you."

I want to thank each of you for carrying Sadako's dream in your heart. I want to also extend a special thanks to Anne Prescott for translating my previous book, *Sadako's Thousand Cranes*, into English for this collaboration. Her generosity and expertise were invaluable in bringing this new work to life.

The Complete Story of
Sadako Sasaki
and the Thousand Cranes

› Chapter 1 ‹

A Most Unusual Arrival

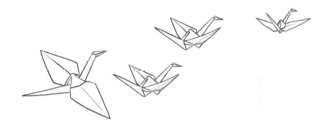

At four o'clock in the morning on January 7, 1943, Mrs. Fujiko Sasaki awoke to an unusual sensation. "The baby's coming!" Fujiko told her husband, Shigeo. "The baby's coming!"

In 1943, women in Japan did not go to the hospital to give birth. Fujiko had planned to be at Shigeo's older sister's house nearby when the time came to deliver the baby. There she could get the help and care she would need. But Fujiko was still at her home above her husband's barbershop, not expecting the baby for many days.

Shigeo jumped out of bed and ran into the street. "*Takayama-san! Takayama-san!*" Shigeo shouted, calling his neighbor. Mr. Takayama rubbed his sleepy eyes and peered out the window to see a dark and empty neighborhood, except for the lone figure of Shigeo.

"What could it be at this hour?" said Mr. Takayama.

"My wife has gone into labor!" Shigeo shouted back. "It is time to go!"

Mr. Takayama, a pedicab driver, had offered to take Fujiko to Shigeo's older sister's home when she was ready. He wasn't expecting it to be at four in the morning! But "*Mukō sangen ryōdonari*," he thought, as he hurried to pedal his pedicab to the Sasakis' front door.

> "*Mukō sangen ryōdonari*" is a common saying and sentiment in Japan. The Japanese believe strongly in respecting their neighbors and helping them in any way they can, even sometimes at great inconvenience. "*Mukō sangen ryōdonari*" translates roughly to mean "Be a good neighbor."

The two men carefully helped Fujiko onto the small seat behind Mr. Takayama. Shigeo gently wrapped his wife in his coat and quickly ran back

A Most Unusual Arrival

inside to call his sister, to let her know that Fujiko was on her way. "How exciting!" she exclaimed. "I'll boil some water and get everything ready." Shigeo knew his wife would be fine in his sister's care while he stayed home with their two-year-old son, Masahiro. Mr. Takayama's pedicab traveled swiftly away from the house and headed down the road toward Shigeo's sister's home, a bit more than three kilometers away.

> In the past, the people of Japan often traveled by rickshaw and pedicab. A rickshaw is a cart with a seat that is pulled by a person on foot, usually running. A pedicab is a type of bicycle. The driver rides in the front, while in the back a small covered cab with two wheels replaces the single wheel of a traditional bike. During Sadako's life, the city of Hiroshima also had a vast streetcar system that many residents rode on a daily basis. While rickshaws and pedicabs are now only hired by tourists wanting to experience this antiquated form of transportation, the city still has a vast network of streetcars in use today.

When the pedicab arrived, Shigeo's sister rushed outside to meet it. As she approached the pedicab, she was surprised to hear the wail of a newborn. Much to her astonishment, when she peeked inside, she saw that Fujiko was holding a tiny baby in her arms, wrapped in Shigeo's coat. Fujiko had given birth in the pedicab! Mr. Takayama had been a pedicab driver for many years. But nothing like this had ever happened before. "I gave birth right there in the pedicab!" Fujiko proudly exclaimed. "I gave birth all by myself!"

Shigeo and Fujiko were elated with the arrival of their first daughter. After Shigeo consulted with a specialist in naming children, they were ready to introduce their precious new baby to the world.

Several days after her birth, Shigeo and Fujiko walked to the river bank, taking turns cradling the newborn in their arms. As the sun set, the sky and surface of the water were dyed a brilliant orange. The colors melted together with the brick military buildings in the distance. "Isn't that beautiful?" Fujiko asked her baby daughter. Sadako was much too young to understand, but peered with wonder into her parents' eyes, comforted by her mother's embrace. As the dancing river flowed in front of them, Shigeo spoke his daughter's name for the first time.

"Your name is Sadako."

A Most Unusual Arrival

The character "*sada*" 禎 means "happiness."

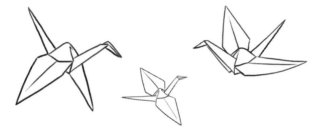

› Chapter 2 ‹

Life in the Midst of War

The world was at war when Sadako was born in 1943. World War II lasted from 1939 to 1945 and involved most of the world's nations. In 1941, the year that Sadako's older brother Masahiro was born, the Japanese had bombed the United States' Pearl Harbor, in Hawaii. The United States declared war on Japan the day of the Pearl Harbor bombing. The date was December 7 in Hawaii, and December 8 in Japan.

A special radio broadcast in Japan announced the surprise attack on the United States' naval base to its citizens. Soon, conflicts broke out all across the Pacific. As the fighting intensified, everyday citizens in both the United States and Japan were called upon to work at weapons plants or fight for their country.

Several months after Sadako's birth, her father received his "red paper," a notice from the Japanese government that he was being recruited to serve in the military. Shigeo was a barber. He had labored long and hard to build a shop and home for his family. Now Shigeo would have to leave everything he worked for to fight in the war.

For the next two years, Sadako and her family continued to live above the family barbershop in Kusunoki-cho, their neighborhood in western Hiroshima city. While Sadako's father was in the military, her mother ran the barbershop on her own.

All over Japan, everyone did what they could to support the war effort and still provide for their families. Raw materials such as metal, oil, rubber, paper, and wood were quickly diverted for military use. Food, clothing, and other life essentials became scarce.

Despite these initial hardships, Sadako and her older brother Masahiro were mostly unaffected by the war at first. Sadako's mother,

Life in the Midst of War

and her father whenever he was home, did their best to hide the difficulties from their young children.

Sadako's grandmother lived with the family as well, often cooking and caring for the children when their mother was working. They were surrounded by love and were not exposed to much of what was going on in the world.

Directly behind their house ran one of many rivers, whose banks provided a perfect playground for Sadako and Masahiro. Streetcars crisscrossed the city. The Sasakis had enough to eat. For now, Hiroshima felt safe to Sadako and Masahiro. And many people in Hiroshima suffered less than the residents of other cities in Japan.

Sadako's father was stationed nearby and would often ride home on his bicycle to see them. He would bring candy that he had bought or bartered for at the army base and showered his children with attention. They loved to take turns riding on the bike with their father, Masahiro straddling the luggage carrier on the back, and tiny Sadako cradled in her father's arms. Sadako was a very thoughtful girl, even at only two years of age, and always wanted Masahiro to get the first ride.

The Complete Story of Sadako Sasaki

Sadako and Masahiro spent their days playing by the river, enjoying the beauty of Hiroshima and the love of their family. Hiroshima Castle, always visible from wherever they played, was a delightful backdrop to their growing imaginations. The enormous wooden castle and surrounding moat, both more than 350 years old, were once the home of the powerful lords of the local provinces. But now, the castle served only as a military base.

Sadako was a helpful child and did her best to look after others, as soon as she could walk and talk. Despite being the older sibling, Masahiro was often mothered and counseled by his younger sister.

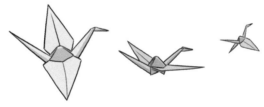

Life was peaceful and mostly quiet for Sadako and her brother. But there was always the possible danger of the neighborhood being bombed, which weighed heavily on the minds of Sadako's mother and grandmother. Air raids became common, and everyone soon learned what to do. At the first sound of the air raid alarm, Sadako took the hand of Masahiro, her

Life in the Midst of War

mother, or grandmother, and walked briskly to the designated shelter.

> During the war, allied countries including the United States dropped many bombs on Japan. The Japanese government ordered the building of shelters throughout Japan to protect its citizens. When alarms rang out to warn residents of planes overhead, the people of Hiroshima made their way to their assigned shelters and waited for an "all clear" alarm before going back to their homes or places of work.

No bombs had ever fallen during an air raid, so Sadako had no fear. She would play games and sing songs with the neighborhood families in the tiny and cramped dugout, waiting to hear the "all clear" signal. Sadako's parents and grandmother worried daily about getting enough food for the children to eat and shielding them from the miserable hardships of war. Sadako and Masahiro were lucky during those days. They did not know hunger and did not understand what they were hiding from in the shelter.

› Chapter 3 ‹

Dark Days Looming

As the battles escalated, many areas of Japan were bombed. Early in the war, most conflicts happened at sea, away from civilians. But as the Japanese troops were increasingly cornered, the bombings moved inland. Civilians were often injured or killed.

All bombs are designed to destroy. In Japan, the destruction of cities was especially severe. Japanese homes were usually made of wood and paper, which easily caught fire and quickly burned down after the bombs hit. Despite efforts to clear paths and make spreading fires less destructive, the embers from these fires blew across the cities, and entire neighborhoods were often left in ruins. Defeat soon felt imminent to many Japanese.

Tokyo was heavily damaged, and 80,000 to 100,000 people had been killed by the bombs dropped there. With few places left to sleep and very little to eat, everyone in Tokyo was frightened.

Meanwhile, in the United States, an even more powerful bomb was being developed. Called the "atomic bomb," it was designed to blow up and burn down entire cities all at once. It also delivered and spread radiation, a horrific side effect. Radiation can't be seen, but it is catastrophic and deadly. Sometimes, radiation immediately kills living things, including plants, animals, and people. Sometimes, it takes its toll later.

By August 1945, Fujiko was increasingly anxious. Hiroshima was one of the few major cities in Japan that had not been heavily bombed. The Americans were flying bomber airplanes over the city almost every night. But they never dropped their explosive cargo on Hiroshima. Each time the bombers flew overhead, the air raid sirens sounded, alerting citizens that enemy planes were in the sky. Everyone could hear the alarms and took cover until the "all clear" signal rang out. For many weeks, each time the air raid warning sounded, the city was spared. Some residents began to grudgingly call the bomber planes "Mr. B," and lived in fear and awe of the giant flying beasts.

Soon rumors flew through the city that Hiroshima would be next and that the Americans had special plans for it. Many residents began to move their most precious belongings to safe zones, hoping they would be spared when the bombing came. Others started sleeping at night in nearby cities, or evacuating altogether, hoping to escape what they feared would happen.

Government officials issued orders to destroy many buildings in the center of the city, focusing on private homes near important public offices or military facilities. They hoped to create firebreaks, which would keep fires contained, and minimize damage from incoming bombs to these critical structures. The people who lived in these homes marked for demolition were forced to move out and had to find new places to live.

› Chapter 4 ‹

The Unthinkable

*E*arly in the morning of August 6, 1945, air raid alarms rang through Sadako's city, alerting the population that an enemy aircraft was overhead. The people of Hiroshima rushed from their homes and took cover. But like so many times before, the plane passed, and no bombs rained down. The people of Hiroshima did not know the aircraft overhead was only checking weather conditions and sending reports by radio back to the generals in charge of the real mission ahead.

When the "all clear" signal rang out, Sadako took Masahiro's hand, and along with all the other residents of Hiroshima, left the air raid shelter. Life went back to normal for the moment.

Sadako and Masahiro sat down for breakfast, and the people of Hiroshima got ready for their day.

While life resumed in the city that morning, three B-29 bomber planes from the United States were heading toward Hiroshima as the sun rose. One plane carried instrumentation needed for the mission. Another was along to take photographs. The third plane, called the *Enola Gay*, carried a single bomb, an atomic bomb. The Americans called it "Little Boy." After hearing that the weather conditions were perfect from the pilot who had flown over the city earlier, the Americans were now on a mission. The mission was to drop "Little Boy" on Hiroshima.

> The B-29 Superfortress bomber aircraft was heavily used in WWII. Made by the Boeing Company in the United States, it was one of the most advanced bombers of its time.
>
> Soldiers named their planes and bombs, to heighten their emotional connection to their mission. The pilot of the *Enola Gay*, Paul Tibbet, named his plane after his mother, Enola Gay Tibbets.

As the Sasaki family sat down for breakfast that morning, they heard yelling in the street. Masahiro, Sadako, and their mother dashed

The Unthinkable

outside. Their neighbors were looking up at the sky and shouted in surprise.

"Look at that!"

"What is it?"

"It's really shiny, isn't it?"

"It's so pretty!"

Fujiko pointed upward in wonder. Masahiro shouted, "That must be an American plane!" They all gazed into the sky.

Sadako's grandmother was not interested in the airplane. "Get back in the house and finish your breakfast," she said. "It's time to eat!" The children and their mother left the gathering crowd in the street.

While Fujiko, Masahiro, and Sadako removed their shoes near the door before hurrying back inside to finish their breakfast, dozens of sparkling, radiant lights twinkled and hung in the early morning air, filling the sky with a magical sparkle, unlike anything they had ever seen before. The beautiful brilliance of the glistening lights overhead transfixed the crowd.

Just as the family sat down at the table, the city lit up with what seemed like the brightness of a thousand suns, followed immediately by an enormous explosion. It sounded like everything in their world was being destroyed. The atomic bomb exploded 600 meters above the ground and blanketed the city with intense heat. A powerful wind swept through the Sasakis' neighborhood and knocked over everything in its path. The *tatami* mats that covered their floors lifted and spun in the air. Bicycles resting in front of their two-story house were suddenly in the backyard. Their home was flattened, their possessions demolished. Nearly every house in sight either collapsed or was on fire or both. Surface temperatures at the hypocenter escalated to 3,000°C to 4,000°C. (The surface temperature of the sun is 5,700°C; iron melts at 1,500°C.) Ceramic tile roofs boiled. Debris rained from the sky.

Sadako was blown into the yard when the house exploded. The rest of the family was trapped under the falling tatami mats and debris from the remains of their home. As Fujiko dug herself out of the ruins, she heard Sadako crying. She rushed toward the cries and found her sitting on a tangerine crate, which moments earlier had been on the second floor of their home. Sadako, unharmed but frightened, was sobbing uncontrollably.

The Unthinkable

Fujiko soon found Masahiro and their grandmother buried beneath the rubble. Masahiro suffered a cut on his head. But it was minor, and he was otherwise fine. All of them were in shock, but safe!

As they collected themselves in the midst of the debris, they wondered what to do. Masahiro looked around for the neighbors that had gathered moments earlier to watch the sparkling lights falling from the sky. They were nowhere to be seen. The Sasaki family saw nothing they recognized. The houses all around them, along with many of their neighbors and all of their belongings, had simply vanished into mounds of unrecognizable ruins.

The family was in shock and, for the moment, unable to fully understand what was happening, overwhelmed by the sights, sounds, and smells around them.

› Chapter 5 ‹

Hell on Earth

As an enormous cloud rose and loomed in the sky over Hiroshima, fire whipped through the streets. The intense heat melted the glass and iron remnants from the homes into smoldering lumps. Bodies were scattered everywhere among the shattered houses. Some residents that survived were unable to move because of their injuries. Others were trapped by debris and could not move. Everyone was in a state of shock, not fully understanding what they were experiencing or where to turn for help.

As the flames engulfed the debris, those that were able were running, walking, and crawling to escape the growing inferno. Those still alive but unable to move were crying out from under the debris. But there was nothing anyone could do to save them. Fujiko knew they must evacuate.

Sadako and Masahiro looked in the direction of Hiroshima Castle as their mother took them by their hands. They were stunned to see that the castle was not there. The shock waves from the bomb had destroyed the castle tower, and almost everything else, as far as the eye could see.

"We have to get away from the fire!" exclaimed Fujiko. "The river! We must go to the river." Shigeo had promised that if ever there was an emergency, he would meet them at Ōshiba Park, their neighborhood rescue center. But with everything in flames, the road was impassable. Fujiko knew they must head toward water to survive.

She grabbed a few barber tools from the rubble of their home and tucked them in her pocket. She hoped that with these, her family might be able to make a small living somewhere in the future. She abandoned everything else.

As the four of them desperately ran away to the river, Sadako's grandmother suddenly turned back. "I forgot some things the children need," she said. "And I must find the *ihai* for Grandpa. I can't leave without it." Fujiko pleaded for her to

Hell on Earth

stay with them and forget about the remembrance tablet for Grandpa. But Sadako's grandmother turned and headed back home, walking toward the increasingly fierce flames. She promised to meet them later at the park. This moment was the last time they would ever see her alive.

> An *ihai* is a remembrance tablet that is often made in Japan when someone dies. It is inscribed with the loved one's name and placed in a household Buddhist altar.

The heat intensified as they walked. The roads were no longer easily passable. Only debris fields remained. Adding to their challenge, they were without their shoes, as was everyone emerging from their homes, making it very difficult to get to safety.

Enormous columns of dust, debris, and heat rose from the ground. The flames became like a tornado and extended many kilometers into the sky above the city. All around were the wailing cries of those suffering. Fujiko shielded her children as best she could so they would not be burned by the fires or trampled by the fleeing crowd.

Sadako clung to her mother as they neared the river. There, Fujiko noticed that a neighborhood acquaintance was coming toward her, rowing a small boat. He shouted to Fujiko to get on board. Fujiko was hesitant. But she saw no other option. Surely they would die if they did not escape the heat.

The boat was scorched by the intense heat rays which had burned a hole in its bottom, allowing water to flow into the tiny hull. When Fujiko and the two children got on board, river water gushed into the boat through the hole, causing the boat to nearly sink. All around them on the river bank, hideously burnt people of all ages clutched at their throats and begged for help. "Please also help the others!" pleaded Fujiko. "Let them get on board!"

"I want to help everyone," the neighbor cried in anguish. "But now we have to think of a way to save only those that can survive." Fujiko was stricken with heartbreaking grief.

Shocked, injured, and terrified neighbors filled the river bank. Dead bodies floated like duckweed in the river. The little boat drifted far away from the shoreline. The sounds of death and destruction slowly retreated. The boat carrying Fujiko and her children bobbed along in stunned silence. Black soot and rain started to fall on their heads. Fujiko covered Masahiro's

Hell on Earth

and Sadako's eyes, trying to protect them from the horrifying sights.

For hours they floated, hoping the heat would lift, and the ash would settle. People on the shore cried out as they passed. "Hey! Let me on the boat!" "I'm begging you! Let me on the boat!" they pleaded. Many of those asking for help were severely injured or burned. Many were children as young as Sadako. Fujiko was tormented by her inability to help. But nothing could be done. The man steering the boat knew that if he took on any more passengers, the boat would sink and they would all die.

Even without more passengers, the boat, damaged by the bombing, began to fill with water leaking in through the hole in the hull. "Bail the water out!" he shouted. "Bail the water out, if you're able!"

Sadako and Masahiro, along with their mother, desperately began to bail the water from the bottom of the boat. Sadako scooped with her small hands and threw the water overboard as quickly as she could, but only managed a few drops at a time. Her mother shouted, "Dog paddle, like this!" The children bent down as their mother showed them and began to paddle the water in great waves out of the boat, helping to keep it afloat.

Exhausted and terrified, Sadako looked up as the sky darkened and then went pitch black. Rain began to fall. Black, sticky rain, like coal tar, poured down, covering her face and body. She did not know the rain was filled with radioactive soot and debris from the bomb. She just knew she was terrified. Sadako's tiny body trembled without stopping. Her teeth chattered. Her lips turned blue. Sadako was colder than she had ever felt and more terrified than words could ever describe.

As the fire ran out of fuel and weakened, the boat headed for the shore, dodging the floating bodies and mangled debris that littered the river. When the boat reached land, Fujiko began to help the injured as she was able. But their acquaintance, the boatman, shouted, "Go! Do not stop to help them or you will end up like them. Save yourself and your children!" Fujiko took Sadako and Masahiro in her arms, shielded them from the falling rain, and headed for the rescue center at Ōshiba Park, leaving the others behind.

When Fujiko and her two children finally reached their destination, conditions were no better. Ōshiba Park had been devastated by the intense rays of heat and enormous blast. Only small, leafless trees remained standing. The black rain did not let up, filling the skies and blanketing the wounded and suffering. Fujiko, Sadako, and Masahiro had nowhere to go and no one to turn to for help.

Fujiko searched the park for the children's grandmother and her husband, Shigeo. The scene was so wretched that the children covered their eyes in horror. Everyone was looking for help. Victims staggered through the crowd, many covered in blood. Some had their skin hanging from their bodies in sheets. Others had shards of debris piercing their torsos and limbs. Many desperately needed medical attention.

Another group of survivors arriving at the park had passed a small farm along the way. They noticed the pumpkins in the field, exposed to the tremendous heat, had cooked on the vine. They collected the pumpkins and shared the small harvest with others gathered at the park.

Cries of pain were heard everywhere, and even some loud voices of anger. Fujiko shouted above them, "Is Shigeo Sasaki here? Is Matsu Sasaki here?" She heard no response as she called out for her husband and mother-in-law.

Just before dusk, a rescue operation truck arrived from a nearby town. The rescuers gave Sadako and her family rice balls and hardtack to eat. Fortunately, the truck was heading to Fujiko's hometown of Kamikawatachi and offered the family a ride. Fujiko did not want to leave without Sadako's grandmother, but she could not find her. They did not yet know she was dead. But Fujiko also worried about her children and wanted to get them to safety. Her parents lived in Kamikawatachi. She knew they would take them in. And her husband surely would look there for them.

> Hardtack are simple biscuits or crackers, made from flour, water, and sometimes salt. They are an inexpensive and long-lasting food, used for sustenance in the absence of perishable foods. They were commonly carried by soldiers and used in military campaigns.

Sadako, Masahiro, and Fujiko were lifted into the back of a military vehicle for the long trip to Kamikawatachi. The children barely noticed the bumpy ride or the belching smoke coming from the charcoal-fueled truck as they ate the hardtack given to them by the military. The three of them were together, and safe at last.

Hell on Earth

Shigeo arrived back in Hiroshima the day after the bombings as part of a rescue team. He soon learned that his family had gone to Kamikawatachi and was staying with Fujiko's parents. Shigeo rushed to be with them.

› Chapter 6 ‹

Surrender and Hardship

On August 7, Japanese radio announced the news of the Hiroshima bombing: "Hiroshima suffered considerable damage as the result of an attack by a few B-29s. It is believed that a new type of bomb was used. The details are being investigated."

Hours earlier, the President of the United States, Harry S. Truman, also made an announcement, acknowledging the arrival of atomic weaponry: "Sixteen hours ago an American airplane dropped one bomb on Hiroshima and destroyed its usefulness to the enemy. That bomb had more power than 20,000 tons of TNT. It had more than two thousand times the blast power of the British 'Grand Slam,' which is the largest bomb ever yet used in the history of warfare."

Three days after the first atomic bomb used during war was dropped on Hiroshima, a second atomic bomb was dropped on another Japanese city called Nagasaki. On August 15, six days after the bombing of Nagasaki, Japan's Emperor Hirohito spoke for the first time on Japanese radio: "After pondering deeply the general trends of the world and the actual conditions existing in our Empire today, I have decided to settle the present situation by resorting to an extraordinary measure…." And with that announcement, Japan surrendered. The war was over.

World War II was the deadliest war in human history. Statistics vary, but it is estimated that more than sixty million people were killed worldwide. Nearly two billion people around the world served their country in the military. More civilians were killed during the war than soldiers, however. It is estimated that two-thirds of the casualties were not in the military of any country.

Sadako's little family was still in shock from the bombing. The surrender hardly mattered to them. They felt nothing but grief and knew they must now prepare for the future as best

Surrender and Hardship

they could. The family eventually learned that Sadako's grandmother had died on the day of the atomic bombing when she returned home. Rescue workers found her body in a cistern next to the house. She most likely attempted to shelter there to avoid the fires but succumbed to the heat and smoke. When the bomb fell on Hiroshima in August, approximately 350,000 people lived in the city. By December 1945, an estimated 140,000 people had died from the atomic bombing. This number included not only those that directly experienced the bomb, but others that were exposed to the deadly black rain which fell throughout the city and many kilometers beyond it, and the rescue crews and medical personnel that rushed to Hiroshima in the days after the bombing. And residents continued to die from the bombing in the years that followed.

Many who did not die fell ill. Both Shigeo and Fujiko suffered from strange symptoms in the coming months. Many neighbors became sick as well. They felt weak and tired. Their hair fell out. Fever and dizziness gripped them for days. "Atomic bomb disease," as it came to be called, was often seen among the surviving residents of Hiroshima. Sadako's parents endured and eventually regained their health. Throughout their illness, they worried about their children, hoping they would not also suffer. Sadako and Masahiro were spared this latest round of misery; both seemed healthy and mostly unscathed from the bombing.

The family soon moved into a small shed once used by the fire brigade, near Fujiko's mother's home. Food was scarce. Sadako and Masahiro often ate small bugs and insects for protein. They especially loved to eat *inago*. With so little food available, Fujiko collected and fried *inago* for the children. Sadako and Masahiro found the smell of the frying rice grasshoppers irresistible and loved to pop them in their mouths.

> *Inago*, also known as rice grasshoppers, were common rice paddy pests in Japan. Large amounts of *inago* could easily be collected using nets.

Neighboring farmers shared their crops as they were able. The family was getting by and holding together. Shigeo began cutting hair in the tiny shed, thankful for the small set of barber tools Fujiko had rescued from the rubble on the day of the bombing. It was a meager living, but he saved money as he could, with the dream that someday they could return to Hiroshima.

Surrender and Hardship

Sadako and Masahiro were soon back to playing and laughing, even in the midst of their difficult existence. One day, during a game of tag, Sadako fell out of a window and gashed her forehead. Even though there was no anesthetic available, she did not flinch or cry when the doctor stitched up the cut. She was becoming a brave girl. She had seen real suffering and endured her small injury without complaint. Sadako was wise beyond her years.

Her parents were impressed by their brave Sadako. But Shigeo also remembered something Sadako's grandmother often said before her death: "Watch out. Only a clever child dies young." But at this time Sadako was only three years old and was the picture of health. Shigeo quickly pushed the thought from his mind. "It's only an old saying," he thought. But every small incident reminded the grown-ups of the terror they had experienced, and of the terror that could lie ahead.

The accident and Sadako's injury did not escape Masahiro's notice either. Not having the perspective of a concerned parent, Masahiro only saw the novelty of it. For years afterward, whenever Sadako and Masahiro fought or quarreled, Masahiro teased and taunted Sadako

› 39 ‹

about her tumble and injury, sometimes calling her "Scarface Sadako."

While the Sasakis worked hard to recover, the city of Hiroshima also struggled to come back to life. About ninety percent of the buildings within two kilometers of the hypocenter were completely destroyed or burned down as a result of the atomic bomb attack. Many of the structures that remained standing also suffered heavy damage.

After the bombing, corpses were everywhere, rotting in the summer heat. Survivors and rescue workers spent their days removing the dead bodies from the streets. Every day, more and more people were dying, so the gruesome task felt never-ending.

The soil of Hiroshima, infused with toxic debris from the raging fires and black rain, could support only limited life.

But there were some small glimmers of hope emerging from the horror. Soon after the atomic bombing, some of the train system resumed service. Not long after that, one short lane of the streetcar system was operational. The city's water pump was also restored, but with so many of the water pipes broken, it was not yet providing water where it was needed.

Surrender and Hardship

By spring, many plants had begun to sprout, including several Chinese Parasol trees, only 1,370 meters from the bomb's epicenter. (These trees were later transplanted to Peace Park in Hiroshima and have become a symbol of emerging life and the resilience of the city.)

Despite the seemingly endless hardships, many people from Hiroshima, including Sadako's family, wanted to return to their hometown. They did their best to prepare. After two difficult years in the tiny shed, the Sasaki family saved enough money to move into a barrack hut in Teppō-chō, a neighborhood in the heart of Hiroshima, in 1947. Shigeo opened a barbershop in the front of their home. Living in their new small dwelling behind a tiny storefront, they found that the necessities of life were still scarce.

Ration books were issued by the government for basic food and supplies, to make sure that everyone was able to buy their share. But even with the rations, many people did not have enough to survive. Stories were told of residents dying of starvation after attempting to live solely on their allotted rations. Waiting in lines for something as simple as rice gruel could sometimes take hours. Shipments were often delayed or canceled. Even with a ration ticket, people found that there was sometimes no food to buy. Soon after the bombing, residents planted small family gardens and grew crops in public spaces, trying to make up for the lack of food. But still, it was not enough to feed the population of Hiroshima. Buying anything without a ticket was illegal, and anyone caught with unauthorized goods would be arrested. Despite this risk, families everywhere survived this way. They could not get by on the meager rations they were allowed and spent many nervous hours hoping not to be caught with their hard-won items.

One day, while visiting Fujiko's hometown, the family managed to secure a large amount of rice without using a ration ticket by trading some clothing and sugar they could spare. Fujiko carefully wrapped the rice in a *furoshiki* and headed home on the train with Sadako and Masahiro. Sadako had never seen such a big pile of rice. She happily sat with the colorful furoshiki in her lap, imagining the feast of a small bowl of rice that awaited her. Her mouth watered in anticipation. "Can we cook some as soon as we get home?" she asked her mother. Fujiko assured her they could and was looking forward to it herself.

Just then, a man from the next train car came through the door next to the Sasaki's seat. "The

Surrender and Hardship

police are coming!" he warned. "The police are coming!" As sometimes happened, the police were checking each passenger car for any items bought without a ration ticket. Fujiko knew she could be arrested for having the rice. She grabbed the rice-filled cloth from Sadako, opened the train window, and threw it from the train.

"No!" shouted Sadako and Masahiro. "Why are you throwing away our rice? We are so hungry!" Times were still hard for Sadako and her family, and often the children were too young to understand. Sadako and Masahiro cried all the way home. But the police did not bother the Sasaki family that day.

> A *furoshiki* is a square cloth used to transport gifts and goods. *Furoshikis* can be any size and are often very colorful. The *furoshiki* had mostly been replaced by the use of paper or plastic bags, but the use of these eco-friendly bags is now encouraged.

Sadako on her first day of elementary school, April 1949

› Chapter 7 ‹

The Bumpy Road to Recovery

Slowly, life got better. In 1948, Sadako's younger sister, Mitsue, was born. Because the economy was improving, the family had a little money to spend on the children. Sadako wore a new blue velvet skirt and jacket to her first day of elementary school in 1949. Her little brother, Eiji, was born in 1950. The family began to take day trips and do more than just survive. They were finally starting to thrive.

One day in August 1950, seven-year-old Sadako, who had always been so healthy, fell ill. Her parents, knowing that many Hiroshima residents were still experiencing after-effects of the bombing, were panic-stricken. Could this be atomic bomb disease? They did not show their concern to Sadako, however. "You're probably catching a cold," Fujiko suggested. "Stay home from school today."

When Masahiro came home later in the day, he looked in on his little sister. She was listless and confused. Masahiro ran into the barbershop. "Dad, something's wrong with Sadako!" he exclaimed.

Shigeo left his work unfinished and went to check on Sadako. "Sadako, are you okay?" he asked. He put his hand on her forehead but felt no fever. Without an elevated temperature, she probably just had a cold. But Shigeo knew it could be something much worse. He ran to a nearby clinic and asked the doctor to come to the house.

The doctor had difficulty with the diagnosis. Sadako, senseless and weak, was unable to get out of bed. "Perhaps feverless pneumonia," the doctor said. "Let's see what the morning brings."

Shigeo was very concerned. He called another doctor. "This is pneumonia without fever. Unfortunately, there is no way to treat it any

The Bumpy Road to Recovery

further," the second doctor told Sadako's parents. "Tonight will be the turning point."

Shigeo and Fujiko stayed up through the night, keeping a close eye on Sadako. By morning, a miracle happened! Sadako awoke feeling as good as new. Her quick and total recovery surprised even the doctor. "This child must have been born with a mission," he said. "Perhaps that's why she was saved this time."

Sadako, on the left, with friends in April 1951

In 1951, Shigeo finally rebuilt his barbershop just the way he had envisioned. The family enjoyed the new living space in the two stories above the shop. Behind their new home and shop was a canned goods factory, which was still in ruins from the bombing. Eight-year-old Sadako and ten-year-old Masahiro spent many hours playing among the rubble and surveyed the bustling city from the top of the pile of debris. Very few tall buildings had been built in the years since the war. Sadako and Masahiro could watch the big cars and jeeps from their perch, driven by the allied soldiers that now occupied the city. They could also see all the way to a building called the Atomic Bomb Dome, many blocks away. Also known as *Genbaku* Dome, the Atomic Bomb Dome was one of the very few buildings left standing near the epicenter of the bombing. Its interior and most of its walls were destroyed when the atomic bomb exploded, leaving only a skeleton of a building behind. (That skeleton remains standing to this day, in memory of the war's casualties, a symbol of the horrors of atomic warfare, and the hope for world peace.)

By 1954, Masahiro was in seventh grade at Nobori-chō Junior High School. Sadako attended sixth grade at Nobori-chō Elementary School. Sadako and Masahiro were now old enough to be helpful around the barbershop and do their share to make the family business prosper. They were put in charge of keeping the entrance and stairwell clean. Sadako was a good, reliable worker. She and Masahiro did their best

The Bumpy Road to Recovery

Sadako with her family in front of the barbershop, June 1954

to make the family barbershop the best one in Hiroshima.

They had many loyal customers. Most of them thought Shigeo was the best barber in town. At last, the Sasakis were happy and looked forward to the future.

After the war, the United States set up a research institute called the Atomic Bomb Casualty Commission. It monitored the effects of the nuclear explosion on the victims in Hiroshima. Every survivor was required to get a complete check-up at the Commission every year. Many Hiroshimans resented this obligation, as the Commission did not treat them for illness, only evaluated their conditions for their research into the effects of the bombing. All residents were forced to remove their clothing while the American medical team took pictures and examined their scars and symptoms. The reserved and modest Japanese found this especially invasive.

The Americans and Allied Nations also stationed military personnel in Hiroshima and throughout Japan. The soldiers were kind to Masahiro and Sadako. They sometimes gave Masahiro and Sadako chocolate and even offered a ride in their jeep to the Institute on the day of their annual exams. The children heard that nearly every family in the United States owned at least one car. This news was fascinating to Masahiro and Sadako. While many of the older residents of Hiroshima had negative feelings about the United States and were suspicious of the soldiers of the Allied Nations, Masahiro and Sadako liked their good nature and the treats they provided. Sadako and her brother dreamed of going to America someday. These were happy days for Sadako.

› Chapter 8 ‹

Joys of Everyday Life

Music became a uniting force in Hiroshima. Popular songs on the radio lifted people's spirits as they rebuilt their lives. Movies and popular culture were making a comeback. Some residents had some leisure time and could finally afford a few simple pleasures. Many citizens of Hiroshima were now able to enjoy an afternoon at the movies, a day trip to the beach, and the comfort of time with their friends and families.

Sadako's family now included four children. The Sasaki home was lively and full of love. The barbershop now employed two young assistants. They often joined the family for meals, and they all went together on day trips to nearby beaches.

The Complete Story of Sadako Sasaki

One day, Shigeo came home from the barbershop with exciting news. One of his customers at the shop was president of the Tōyōza Movie Theater in Hiroshima. He told Shigeo he wanted to invite Sadako and Masahiro to see a singer and actress named Hibari Misora in concert at the theater. Two of her biggest hit songs, "Tokyo Kid" and "*Ringo Oiwake*," played on the radio all day long. Hibari Misora was Sadako's favorite singer and actress. Now she would get to hear her sing in person!

On the day of the concert, Masahiro took Sadako by the hand as they made their way to the concert hall. After going through a back door, they tried to get as close as they could to the stage. But the crowds were huge and very excited. Sadako couldn't see Hibari Misora at all. She was so disappointed. But just then, Masahiro lifted up Sadako and sat her on his shoulders. There she was! Hibari Misora, only a few meters away, was singing Sadako's favorite songs. Sadako rocked to the beat on Masahiro's shoulders. "Wow!" Sadako shouted to Masahiro. "It's Hibari! There's Hibari!" Sadako could hardly believe her good fortune. All the way home, Masahiro and Sadako sang all the songs they had heard that night. Happiness filled their world. Life was good and getting better.

Joys of Everyday Life

Sadako was a popular student. She loved sports. She was the fastest runner in her class, and also excelled at the pole vault. Her nickname was "Monkey" because she was so nimble and had such quick reflexes. She did well in school and dreamed of becoming a physical education teacher when she grew up.

Many schools in Hiroshima struggled to return to normal after the war. Coal boxes and tangerine crates became desks, classes were often held outdoors, and the school grounds were used to grow sweet potatoes and other vegetables in the first years after the bombing. Reconstruction began in 1951, but for a few years some classes were still held outdoors, or in partitioned auditoriums, as the entire school was being rebuilt. Many students had lost parents during the bombing or soon afterward. They suffered from inadequate housing and didn't always have the essentials they needed.

When Sadako started sixth grade in Mr. Nomura's class, she was worried. His nickname around the school was "Blue Demon." Sadako thought this name sounded scary and she feared she would not be happy in his class. But very soon she discovered he was kind and interested in his students' success. Mr. Nomura worked hard to bring harmony and happiness to his class. If any student told him they didn't have enough food at home to bring a sack lunch, Mr. Nomura found clever ways to make sure they got what they needed.

Mr. Nomura thought Sadako's class lacked unity because of their years of hardship. After they had come in last place in the school's Spring Sports Day relay race, Mr. Nomura had an idea. He decided to make sure his students were prepared to win the race next Sports Day. "We'll practice so your hearts beat as one," he told his students. "Then you will pass the baton in rhythm with your heartbeats."

Every day after school Mr. Nomura led the class as they trained and practiced. Sadako loved to run. She was thin, nimble, and faster than anyone in her class. Sadako could run fifty meters in 7.5 seconds! She and her classmates worked hard to improve their skills. They even went to Mr. Nomura's house on Sundays to play tag, dig for clams, and bond as a team. Months later, when Fall Sports Day arrived, they were ready.

On October 15, 1954, Sadako was excited and ready to participate in Fall Sports Day. She did not eat or drink before the race and went to the bathroom many times to lighten her body weight. She was very nervous as her team

Joys of Everyday Life

prepared to go to the starting line. Sadako would carry the baton last, so she had to wait as her classmates took their turns. Finally, the race was about to begin. At the sound of the pistol, the first runners took off. Sadako watched with excitement as they rounded the track. The girl that would hand her the baton was in second place as she got closer, but she was gaining on the boy in front. Sadako's teammate handed over the baton and Sadako, barefoot, took off. She ran as fast as she could, and was close to the one in the lead. Sadako's family was in the bleachers, cheering her on. "Go, Sadako!" Fujiko called out. "Hold on to the baton tightly!"

Sadako, at left, practices for the relay race, September 1954

"Monkey! Just a little more! You're gaining on him!" shouted her classmates. Sadako passed the front-runner and crossed the finish line first! Sadako and her class were thrilled. They had won the Fall Sports Day relay race! Mr. Nomura's idea had worked. The class was now united.

Even after Sports Day, Sadako and her class were good friends and continued to train together. A few weeks later, they took a field trip to Miyajima Island and climbed Mount Misen. Sadako raced her classmates to the top. She was so fast that she was among the first group of girls to reach the peak.

Everywhere Sadako looked she saw smiling faces. Memories of the horrors and hardships she had endured were beginning to fade. The war was behind her now. She looked forward to many things and had dreams for the future. Graduation from elementary school was only a few months away. Soon she would join Masahiro at the junior high school. Sadako was very happy.

› Chapter 9 ‹

A Different Kind of Pain

The city of Hiroshima was growing, and many new businesses were opening around the barbershop. One afternoon, the owner of the dry cleaners next door stopped by to ask Shigeo for help. "We are in a difficult situation and need a loan to save our business," he said. "But we have no property to offer the bank as collateral and need someone to co-sign the loan for us. Can you help?"

"*Mukō sangen ryōdonari*," Shigeo thought. He was only recently feeling back on his feet himself, but could not turn down a neighbor in need. It was his duty to help. Shigeo agreed to sign the loan papers with his neighbor. By doing so, it meant if the neighbor did not repay, Shigeo would be responsible for repaying the loan. Shigeo trusted that the neighbor was true to his word and would repay every *yen* on time.

Despite Shigeo's confidence in them, the neighbors were not honest. Soon after agreeing to help, the owners of the dry cleaners left town in the middle of the night and took the loan money with them. They abandoned their promise to Shigeo and left him solely responsible for the loan.

Shigeo did not have extra money. Every *yen* he made went to support his growing family. The loan had been given by a loan shark, and he did not tolerate late payments. Shigeo struggled to keep up.

As Shigeo was cutting hair one afternoon in his busy shop, a well-dressed man with many scars on his face barged into the shop, demanding money and an immediate payment on the loan. Shigeo had fallen behind in the payments.

"Hey, Sasaki," he growled.

"I told you not to come here," Shigeo said softly.

A Different Kind of Pain

The customers in the barbershop, frightened by the loan shark, slipped out the door, even the customer that was in the middle of getting a haircut. Sadako, Masahiro, and Fujiko were frightened as well.

Another man entered the shop, and the two thugs surrounded Shigeo. "It doesn't matter what you say. You'll pay us what we're due. Well, how about it? Do you have the money?" The loan shark spoke calmly but made it clear they were carrying weapons and were ready to use them if Shigeo did not give them their money.

"I'll pay you back, but can it wait?" Shigeo pleaded.

Fujiko whispered to Sadako and Masahiro to come with her, escorting them to the back of the house. But the children could still see into the barbershop and watched in fear as their father negotiated with the debt collectors.

"We'll wait, but you need to pay us back soon," the two men insisted. One of the men took a ceramic dish used for shaving soap off the shelf. "What should I do with this?" He sneered and then slammed the soap dish to the floor, shattering it into pieces.

Fujiko let out a scream. "Stop! I'm begging you! Please stop!"

Sadako squeezed Masahiro's arm and gritted her teeth. She was scared and frustrated.

The loan shark looked at Fujiko and the children. "We'll go now. But you will pay us soon." Then they were gone.

Word spread in the neighborhood that Shigeo was in trouble, and that dangerous men were visiting his shop. A frightened Shigeo could not come up with the amount of money they were demanding. He scraped together as much as he could and gave it to Masahiro and Sadako to deliver. Tears streamed down his face. "Take this money," he told his children. "Pay them back." He knew the loan shark would not harm Sadako and Masahiro, and he hoped the smaller payment would at least keep them out of his shop.

In front of the barbershop, 1954

A Different Kind of Pain

Sadako and Masahiro rode the streetcar across town to the loan shark's office. The children were frightened but brave. Masahiro handed the money to the men. "Our father sent us to pay you," he said. One of the men ripped the money from Masahiro's hands. He gave it to the scar-faced man, who quickly counted the small stack of bills. "This is not enough!" he boomed. "Is this all you have? Where is my money? Did you hear what I said?"

The men were furious now, shouting at Sadako and Masahiro, hoping to scare more money from them. The children were frozen in place. Tears began to flow down their cheeks.

But even the loan sharks were moved by the children's fear. "Go home!" they shouted. "Next time, this won't be enough!"

With tears streaming down her face, Sadako stood up for her father with all her might. "Our father isn't a thief!" she shouted. "He isn't a bad guy!" She and Masahiro backed toward the door.

They turned and ran as fast as they could back home. Sadako hoped the men would go away. She wished the debt could be repaid. She wanted everything to be better.

But as the weeks went by, things got worse. Shigeo was unable to pay his taxes. Many of his

The Complete Story of Sadako Sasaki

customers were afraid to come to the shop, fearful the loan shark might visit while they were there. His income dropped. Some household possessions were seized to pay the taxes. Fujiko began to take in sewing work to help make ends meet. But it was not enough to repay the loan.

Winter vacation at the home of relatives, December 1954

› Chapter 10 ‹

Devastating News

When winter vacation arrived, Sadako went to her aunt's house for a visit. She was happy to see her cousins and relieved to get away from the loan collectors at home.

When Sadako arrived, she had what she thought was a mild cold. Her aunt said her chin and jaw looked swollen and was worried that it might be something more serious. "Sadako doesn't look well," she said to Shigeo. "I wonder if it is because she was there during the *pikadon*." She was aware of the potential of sickness from the bomb attack years before.

"Don't say that!" Shigeo cried. "No. It's been ten years since *pikadon*. She just has a cold." But fear gripped him.

> *Pika* means "brilliant light," and *don* means "boom." *Pika* and *pikadon* are how the survivors refer to the atomic bombing. "Atomic bomb disease" is what they often called leukemia and the other illnesses that followed. *Hibakusha* is the word for people who were exposed to radiation from the atomic bombing. *Hibakusha* was later also used to describe victims of radiation caused by both atomic and hydrogen bomb test fallout, and nuclear power plant accidents. The word is the same, but the Japanese characters for these two meanings are different.

Sadako hardly ever got sick. But this time, her symptoms wouldn't go away. She complained of a sore throat and developed lumps around her jawline and behind her ears. The lumps grew larger, and her face began to swell. Her mother thought Sadako might have the mumps or tonsillitis. When Sadako did not get better, her father thought it was time for her to see the doctor.

Dr. Hatagawa, Sadako's physician, was also a customer at Shigeo's barbershop. He knew Sadako and the family well. After he examined

Devastating News

Sadako, he was very concerned and asked to speak privately to her parents. Because Sadako had been exposed to the atomic bomb, he thought her symptoms might be a sign of atomic bomb disease.

Although it had been years since the bombing, many people still fell ill with the dreaded disease. New cases of leukemia were diagnosed among the *hibakusha* on a regular basis. Some victims were even born after the bombings, suffering from the effects of the radiation on their mothers.

Fujiko thought Sadako couldn't possibly have leukemia. Sadako had just passed her physical exam at the Atomic Bomb Casualty Commission in June. She would have been sent for treatment elsewhere if the doctors had found anything suspicious.

But Dr. Hatagawa was insistent. The lumps around Sadako's jawline were not shrinking. Sadako was not getting better. Dr. Hatagawa thought Sadako needed to go to the Atomic Bomb Casualty Commission for another checkup right away.

Shigeo and Fujiko were very anxious, but they tried not to let Sadako see their concern. They made an appointment for her at the Commission as soon as they were able. Over the course of two visits, on January 18 and February 16, 1955, Sadako was subjected to a complete exam. The results brought terrible news.

Dr. Hatagawa called Shigeo on February 18 and asked him to come to his clinic immediately. When Shigeo arrived, the doctor took him into a consulting room to share Sadako's test results. Her white blood cell count was 33,000, which was more than five times higher than normal. Her red blood cell count was also far outside the expected range for a healthy person. Malignant cells were found in her blood as well. Dr. Hatagawa told Shigeo he believed Sadako was suffering from *pika*, caused by radiation from the atomic bombing so many years ago. She needed to be admitted to the hospital for more tests as soon as possible.

Shigeo was shocked and terrified. In 1955, leukemia was incurable. The doctor confirmed that Sadako might have only months to live, a year at the most. Shigeo, consumed with grief, did not want to believe his daughter had such a horrible, incurable disease.

› Chapter 11 ‹

Holding on to Happiness

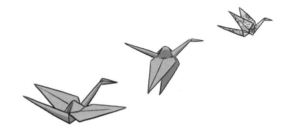

When Shigeo came home, he told Fujiko the dreadful news. She was devastated and felt a need to do anything she could for Sadako. They both wanted to stay positive and not focus solely on Sadako's terrible condition. What could they do to make Sadako happy? Fujiko and Shigeo had an idea. They would make Sadako her first dress-up *kimono*, to take her mind off the looming hospital stay.

Because of the loan obligation the neighbor had left them with, the Sasakis were in deep financial trouble. But they would now sacrifice anything to see Sadako happy. They collected the few coins they had saved for an emergency and committed to spending them on a *kimono* for Sadako.

Shigeo placed the coins in his pocket and walked to the school to pick up Sadako. She was surprised to see her father. "Why did you come to get me before the school day is over?" she asked. "Am I sick?" Not wanting her to be sad or frightened, Shigeo lifted Sadako in the air and supplied a piggyback ride. It had been a long time since he had carried her that way. But Sadako welcomed the close contact with her father. She was so lightweight and thin. Suddenly aware of her frailty, Shigeo recalled the words of the doctor: "At most, one year to live."

Luckily, Sadako could not see that his eyes were welling with tears. He told her that the doctor had determined that her condition was nothing serious. "It's really nothing," he told her. "But the doctor said that it would be a good idea to run some more tests. So you'll need to be in the hospital for a bit." He assured her that after a brief stay in the hospital she would begin to feel better. And, he had a big surprise for her! Before going to the hospital, they would get her a new dress-up *kimono*.

Sadako had always wanted a *kimono*. But she knew her family did not have money to spend on such things. She worried about how much it would cost, and why her parents suddenly thought today was a good day for *kimono* shopping. But when her father took her to Kotobuki-ya, the famous *kimono* fabric shop in Hiroshima, she forgot her worry and looked for the most beautiful fabric she could find. After looking at all the choices in the store, she selected an elegant material with a delicate cherry blossom design. It was perfect! Sadako was so full of joy. Getting a new dress-up *kimono* took her mind off her upcoming hospital stay.

Sadako's aunt, an expert seamstress, offered to help Fujiko make the *kimono*. Shigeo and Fujiko decided to pack up the entire family and go to visit Sadako's aunt. After arriving by train, the children ate their dinners, visited with their aunt, and played games with their cousins. Soon, it was time for bed. While the children slept, Fujiko, Sadako's aunt, and her oldest cousin worked through the night to sew the *kimono* for Sadako. As Sadako's aunt sewed, Fujiko told her the details of Sadako's condition. Each stitch was blurred by tears, as they all thought about Sadako's situation. Each stitch became a labor of love and contained a wish of wellness for Sadako.

Finally, as morning approached, the *kimono* was finished.

Early the next day, Sadako awoke and sleepily shuffled into the main room of the house. To her surprise, there hung her exquisite *kimono*, just as she had always dreamed. Sadako burst into tears. She was worried the family had gone through too much trouble and expense. Fujiko soothed Sadako's worries and asked her to model her new outfit. Sadako was a little shy with everyone watching. She dried her tears as she tried on the garment. Sadako then slid on the Japanese *zori* sandals and clutched the new small purse her family also managed to buy for her. She felt so beautiful and grown up. "Sadako, you're so lucky!" exclaimed her little sister, Mitsue. "I want a *kimono*, too!"

Sadako loved her new *kimono*. She thought of her sixth-grade graduation party that was coming up in March. Sadako looked forward to wearing it there, and at every other opportunity.

But first, she would need more tests. Shigeo took her to Hiroshima Citizens Hospital on February 19. Sadako's white blood cell count had increased to more than 44,000. The doctor told Shigeo and Fujiko that Sadako needed to be admitted to the Red Cross Hospital, which

Sadako, after the farewell party with her classmates, in the schoolyard of Nobori-chō Elementary School, March 1955

was later renamed the Hiroshima Red Cross Hospital & Atomic-bomb Survivors Hospital since so many people who suffered from the bombing were treated there.

On the walk home, Shigeo began to prepare Sadako for the experience, assuring her that the doctor would help her feel better. These comforting words made Sadako happy. She looked forward to getting treatment and recovering from her sickness.

Because Sadako did not want to miss any lessons, she asked if they could stop by the school to pick up her books. The class was on the field when she arrived, practicing for the next relay race. When they saw Sadako walk onto campus, they all rushed over to greet her, including Mr. Nomura. "Sadako is sick," Shigeo explained, "and she's going to be in the hospital for a little while."

"Get well soon!" her classmates said. Sadako fought back her tears and struggled to put on a happy face.

"Sadako, come back soon!" they shouted and waved as Sadako walked out the gate.

› Chapter 12 ‹

Treatment Begins

On February 21, Sadako was admitted to Hiroshima Red Cross Hospital. The more rigorous tests had confirmed and accurately identified her illness. Sadako was suffering from subacute lymphocytic leukemia. Still a very deadly form of cancer today, many people who receive aggressive treatment now survive this disease and go on to live healthy and full lives. But in 1955, subacute lymphocytic leukemia was a death sentence. Still, no one told Sadako she would not survive her illness. They wanted her final days to be as cheerful and hopeful as possible.

Several weeks into her hospital stay, Sadako was not improving. Her doctor was doing everything he could to slow the advance of her disease. She received many blood transfusions and powerful drug injections to help return her blood count to normal. Sadako never complained about the painful treatments, and never once cried out. She endured each procedure with courage and kept her focus on getting well and returning to school.

Despite her show of strength, Sadako was anxious about the cost of her hospitalization. She knew her parents had very little money, and what little money they did have was going to pay back their neighbor's loan. The Sasakis were now covering their neighbor's debt and paying for Sadako's expensive treatments, as well as bearing the costs of raising a young family and maintaining the barbershop.

Shigeo and Fujiko told Sadako to focus on feeling better and not to worry. She promised to think only of getting well, but she knew the burden was heavy. Her hospital stay cost more than double the salary of the average Japanese worker. Sadako knew her parents were struggling to pay their many bills.

When she felt well enough, her doctor allowed Sadako to go home on the weekends. It was a welcome break from the boredom of the hospital. Sadako played with her younger siblings and helped them with their homework. She enjoyed the everyday things of home life, which she was missing in the hospital.

One weekend when she was home, the loan shark came to the house, looking for more money and threatening terrible things. Sadako became more worried than ever about the cost of her treatment and the tremendous burden she was to her family. Suddenly, the hospital felt more comforting and safe.

Sadako listened to music to take her mind off her illness and the family's money problems. Hibari Misora was still her favorite singer. She spent many hours singing along with her songs and remembering the happy time with Masahiro at the concert. When she heard nurses and other patients listening to Hibari Misora and other singers she liked, Sadako made friends with them. Soon, she had many friends at the hospital.

When Mr. Nomura told Sadako's classmates that she was undergoing treatment for leukemia, they took turns visiting her, in groups of three or four, nearly every day. Each one did their best to cheer her up. None of them told her she had leukemia. They all wanted her to remain upbeat and free of anxiety during her treatment. Many of her classmates were also in Hiroshima at the time of the bombing. Sadako's illness was a reminder to them of their own vulnerability to the dreaded atomic bomb disease. Many of them worried they might be the next ones to fall ill.

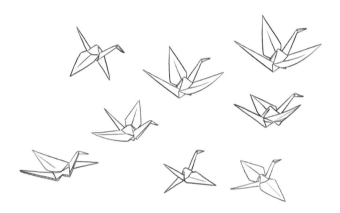

› Chapter 13 ‹

Graduation

*B*y the middle of March, 1955, Sadako had been in the hospital for nearly three weeks. She was looking forward to going to her sixth-grade party and graduation. She wanted to wear her new dress-up *kimono* and see her friends. Her doctor, who understood the importance of the event, allowed Sadako to leave the hospital to attend. When her classmates saw her arrive at the party, they gave her a seat of honor. She watched joyfully with her mother as her classmates sang and performed skits. But Sadako soon found that she was too tired and weak to manage such an eventful outing. After a short time, she thanked her friends, said goodbye, and returned to the hospital. Her father went to the graduation ceremony and collected her diploma for her. Sadako's classmates gave her two *kokeshi* dolls and a small notebook they had signed as a graduation gift. The dolls rested on her nightstand at the hospital and kept her company for the remainder of her long stay.

Sadako's hospital nightstand

Soon after graduation, her classmates began junior high school. Sadako was enrolled but could not attend. Some of her friends visited her after the first day at their new school. Sadako wanted to hear all about it and imagine herself there. She wondered what her homeroom was like, and was worried about keeping up with the school work. She kept her new textbooks in her hospital room and asked her friends many questions about their

Graduation

new school and classes. The other children knew Sadako would never be well enough to attend, so they were careful with their answers. Many students told her that junior high school was a bore, or that elementary school was better, in the hope that Sadako would not worry so much about what she was missing.

Sadako at the Red Cross Hospital entrance, August 1955

› Chapter 14 ‹

Hospital Life

By April, the intense treatments Sadako was receiving were beginning to pay off. Her blood count numbers were improving. She had a little more energy than before. Sadako's family felt happy for the first time since her diagnosis and hoped her improved state would continue.

Fujiko did her best to spend as many hours with Sadako as possible. This sort of attentiveness is the Japanese way. When a member of the family is sick or wounded, others in the family tend to their needs by cooking for them, reading to them, and offering comfort and companionship. But Sadako realized her mother had three more children at home, each needing her as well. Fujiko was not always able to be at the hospital. Sadako understood, but it didn't stop her from feeling lonely and longing for her family when they were unable to be with her.

To keep herself busy, she sat at the nurses' station and visited with them and the patients who passed by. She loved to bring her school books and study on her own at the nurses' big desk each day.

Sadako also made friends with a young boy whose room was across the courtyard. Even when she was too sick to visit the nurses' station, Sadako discovered she and the boy could signal each other using the light from their windows, by reflecting it onto little mirrors they each had as part of their hospital kit. This became her sole entertainment for many hours, as the reflections from the boy's mirror danced across her ceiling, and she replied by sending her own twinkling lights his way.

Sadako was moved to a double room in May. At last, she had a roommate, someone to keep her company when her friends and family were not able to be with her. Kiyo Ōkura, in the hospital recovering from tuberculosis, was two years older than Sadako. She liked reading romance novels

Hospital Life

and girls' magazines and writing letters. At first, Kiyo thought Sadako was young and silly, and she had little time for her. Even before they became roommates, Kiyo had seen Sadako in the hospital and was mystified why anyone would smile so happily and play so cheerfully with the other children while hospitalized. Kiyo tired of Sadako's giggling and shouting back and forth with the boy across the courtyard. "Sadako, be quiet," she would scold. "I am reading! You're in junior high now. Why don't you read a book?" Sadako, on the verge of adolescence, apologized and knew she wanted to be more grown-up like Kiyo. Sadako quickly embraced Kiyo's interests and began to call her "*o-nē-chan*," the Japanese word for "older sister." Kiyo soon warmed up to Sadako, and the two had much to discuss and share.

One day, Sadako asked to borrow one of Kiyo's magazines. In the back was a page full of advertisements from girls looking for pen-pals. Sadako requested a pen and paper and sent her information to the magazine. In the next issue, a small notice appeared:

> *Send me letters. Sadako Sasaki, 2nd Floor, Red Cross Hospital, Hiroshima City*

Soon she began to receive letters, and she spent many hours writing back to other girls throughout Japan. She often revealed many of her thoughts and worries not shared with her family.

> Dear pen-pal Michiko,
>
> I'm sorry this letter is so late. I'm doing fine. On February 21st I was hospitalized at the Red Cross Hospital. Every day three or four of my classmates come to visit me, so I'm not bored. I haven't been home much since I was hospitalized, so I suppose there have been changes in the town.
>
> The other day, on February 20th, we had a big snowfall and the roof of a house on Main Street caved in. We heard about it on the radio, so Mom and I went to see it. They said if it had happened a little earlier, someone would have died. It was about 9:00 pm when the roof on the house on Main Street fell in. After the snowfall, a woman who was about 20 years old got run over by a car in front of the Chugoku Bank and died.
>
> Changing the subject, on February 28th, which was after I was hospitalized, I got a blood transfusion in my hand, and it hurt a lot. The doctor said that when you get sick if it doesn't hurt a little, you won't get better. It's okay if it hurts a bit if it means I'll get better soon, and I can probably visit you over spring vacation. Let me know if this is a convenient time for you. But, if the doctor says I have to stay a little longer, I might not be able to come.
>
> Please take care of yourself, and please write to me. I'm looking forward to hearing from you. Sayonara.
>
> From Sadako Sasaki

Hospital Life

Throughout her stay, Sadako became friends with more and more of the children who were patients at Hiroshima Red Cross Hospital. Some were there for short stays, recovering from sickness or accidents. Some, like Sadako, were victims of the dreaded atomic bomb disease. Sadako made friends with everyone. When she was feeling able, she continued to visit with the nurses and ventured out of her room to visit with her many friends among the other patients. Sadako learned new things from them and shared her adventures with Kiyo. One day, she even took Kiyo to the hospital's kitchen, where they made boiled cabbage with soy sauce. Another patient had told Sadako it was delicious, and she wanted to see for herself. It was! Kiyo was shy and learned from Sadako how to be more comfortable making new friends and trying new things.

Sadako, on the left, with her roommate Kiyo, at the entrance to the Red Cross Hospital, August 1955

Rooming with Kiyo made everything better for Sadako. Her treatments seemed easier. And she had someone to talk to, especially about boys and her other new interests. A medicine newly developed in America seemed to be stabilizing her white blood count. Sadako was feeling better and thought she might be well soon. Everything was looking up for Sadako.

› Chapter 15 ‹

All Pain, No Gain

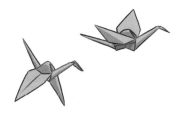

Shigeo and Fujiko were careful not to let Sadako see their great sadness over her condition. And they worked hard to shield Sadako from the financial difficulties they were facing. But the barbershop was struggling since the incident with the loan sharks. And the loan their neighbors had taken out was still not repaid.

Sadako's parents worked hard but only earned 800 *yen* each day. At the time, this was the equivalent of $2.22 in American dollars. With three other growing children at home, this barely covered their basic living expenses, much less Sadako's medical bills. The Japanese national health insurance program had not yet been implemented. If you couldn't pay for your medicine, you could not get treatment. One transfusion of healthy blood cost 800 *yen*, an entire day's pay for the Sasakis. One dose of the medicine to relieve pain was 2,100 *yen*, almost three days' work for Shigeo and Fujiko.

Sadako and Shigeo, shortly before the Hiroshima Peace Memorial Ceremony at Peace Park, August 6, 1955

Sadako's parents did their best to hide their financial troubles, but Sadako was a very thoughtful girl and paid close attention to her family. One day in May, Shigeo showed up to

All Pain, No Gain

visit her in the hospital. His wristwatch was missing, and Sadako knew he had sold it for cash to pay their bills. Shigeo loved his wristwatch, so Sadako knew their situation was dire. One by one, everything of value began to vanish for the same reason. Sadako decided she would hide her suffering and refuse all pain medications, not wanting to burden the family with the overwhelming costs. She assured them the drugs would only prolong her recovery, something she wanted to believe herself.

One night, Masahiro overheard his parents discussing Sadako. "Sadako looks like she is in a lot of pain," Shigeo said.

Fujiko nodded. "That's what the doctor said, too."

Shigeo wanted to do something. "Maybe we should increase the medicine and transfusions she is receiving."

"We should. But we don't have the money this week to pay for it," Fujiko replied in a low voice.

Shigeo, usually a quiet and gentle man, pounded his fist into a pillar in the living room. "I know, I know," he sputtered. "But there's nothing I can do."

› Chapter 16 ‹

Lost in the Stars

With their debts mounting, Sadako's parents were forced to sell their house to pay their bills. On May 28, the doctor gave Sadako permission to leave the hospital and spend one last night in the home where she had lived for four happy years. She had many memories of better times there with her parents, brothers, and sister. She was so excited to remember those days, to be with her family, and return to her old life, even if only for one night. But she worried that the expense of her treatments was a big part of her family's financial troubles.

On May 30, the family moved to a small shack in a poor neighborhood a short distance away. Sadako returned to the hospital, hoping her health would continue to improve. She looked forward to living in the new house with her family soon, no matter how tiny and inadequate it was.

But as the doctor feared, Sadako's condition again began to worsen. By June, she was sicker than ever. Her doctor thought the trips home were too stressful, and they confined her to the hospital.

Purple spots began to appear all over Sadako's body. Sadako wrapped her spots with bandages so no one could see them and worry about her. But she was concerned about her health and wondered if she would get better as everyone had promised.

One day while visiting her friends around the hospital, Sadako met a young girl named Yuki. She was only six years old, born after the war ended. Sadako was surprised to learn that Yuki was suffering from leukemia, even though she was not alive when Hiroshima was bombed. Her doctor believed that because her parents were both exposed to the bomb's radiation, she too was susceptible to the disease. Sadako noticed Yuki's symptoms and thought they were the same as her own. She wondered if she too had the dreaded atomic bomb disease. As Yuki grew sicker, she became so weak she could not get out of bed. Soon, she could not eat. Yuki was dying. Sadako visited her often and worried about her. She worried about her own symptoms and condition, too.

When Yuki passed away, Sadako and Kiyo, following Japanese tradition, went to pay their respects. Yuki's lifeless body was covered with purple spots, the same spots Sadako had seen on her own body. Sadako was gripped with fear. "I wonder if I'm going to die like that," she said to Kiyo. They both cried as Kiyo gave Sadako a big hug and assured her she would not.

Kiyo was shocked at how thin Sadako was when she hugged her. "Sadako knows what illness she has," thought Kiyo.

Sadako was strong about her condition. But after Yuki's death, she often quietly asked the nurses about her future. "Am I going to die like that?" she would ask. "It's my turn next, isn't it?" She heard the nurses say that a white blood count number over 100,000 meant the patient would die. And that is what happened to Yuki.

Sadako was sitting at the nurses' station one afternoon, visiting and studying with her school books on her own. "Beep! Beep!" One of the call buttons had been activated in someone's room.

A patient somewhere was calling for a nurse. "I'm going to check," the nurse told Sadako. "I'm leaving you in charge, okay?"

"Sure," replied Sadako. She had been left alone at the nurses' station many times before. As she sat back to wait for the nurse's return, she noticed a drawer in the desk had been left open. Inside were all the patients' charts, with Sadako's right on top. "I wonder what my chart says?" thought Sadako. She couldn't resist. She pulled the pile of papers from the drawer and quickly opened the folder. Many pages were written in what Sadako thought might be English. She could not read them. But then, in the middle of the many notes about her, she found the results of her blood cell count test. The numbers when she was first hospitalized were there, along with all the tests she had taken since then. Sadako quickly grabbed a small scrap of paper and copied the numbers from the chart. Her white blood cell count had gone up and down with treatment but was now at 50,000. Sadako knew this number was very high. She had suspected something horrible was wrong with her. She felt this confirmed it.

Sadako slid the chart back into the drawer just as the nurse came around the corner. "Thank you for watching the station," the nurse said with a smile.

Lost in the Stars

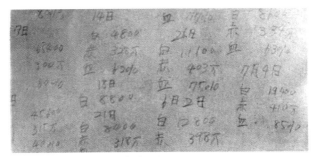
Sadako's notes

Sadako left the nurses' station, slipped the scrap of paper under her mattress, and then went up to the roof. She lost track of time as she sat and stared at the city below her. Soon darkness fell, and the sky overhead was full of twinkling stars.

As she gazed to the heavens, she thought of Yuki, and her grandmother, and all the others that had died as a result of the bombing. She now feared she would soon join them. Sadako's mind swirled with questions. "What will happen when I die? Will it be painful? Who will remember me?" Mature beyond her years, Sadako soon turned to thoughts of others. "How can I help my family? What can I do to make the world a better place while I am still alive?" Swept into the wonder of the universe above, stoic Sadako resolved to face her own death with courage, and do what she could to lift the burden of her illness from her family.

Inside the hospital below, the nurses panicked. "Where is Sadako?" they asked each other. No one had seen her in several hours, and now it was dark outside. Every patient and every nurse was questioned. No one knew where she had gone. One of the nurses, Miss Yasunaga, went up the stairs to the roof to get a wider view of the hospital grounds, hoping she could spot Sadako. Much to her shock, as she stepped onto the roof, there sat Sadako in her hospital gown, all alone in the dark. "What are you doing here?" exclaimed Miss Yasunaga. "You must go back to your room! Come with me."

"People become stars when they die, don't they?" Sadako replied dreamily, as she gazed at the twinkling lights above.

Miss Yasunaga looked at Sadako, who was shivering from the cool night air. She moved beside her and looked up. "I wonder if one of those stars is Yuki," she replied.

Sadako was silent for a moment. "The atomic bomb was really scary," she said.

Miss Yasunaga reached out and hugged Sadako. "You must be chilly," she said. "Let's go back." Gently she guided Sadako downstairs, realizing that she knew her fate.

After that night, Sadako became quieter and stayed in bed. The boy across the courtyard had been discharged, leaving her without his dancing mirror reflections during the long days in bed. Kiyo teased Sadako, thinking it was "young love" and she was just missing him. But Sadako had other things on her mind.

The small spots on her body were growing into larger ones. She struggled to walk. A constant dull pain throbbed in her bones, and she was becoming weaker. "Sadako," her mother pleaded. "Let me carry you on my back." She couldn't bear to watch her struggle. But Sadako refused.

"I have to walk," Sadako explained cheerfully. "If I don't, I won't be able to walk anymore." She hid her pain and apprehension.

When she was strong enough, Sadako lingered in the hall and waited for the nurses to be called away. When they were gone, she took a peek at her chart and copied her latest blood count numbers onto the small slip of paper that she kept under her mattress. Sometimes her white blood count was very high, but sometimes it was much lower. She tried to convince herself that maybe she didn't have leukemia at all. Maybe if she fought hard, she would beat it. Sadako hoped for a miracle.

› Chapter 17 ‹

Dreams Take Flight

On August 3, Sadako was lying in bed when a nurse came by with a long string of colorful cranes folded for the patients by the Red Cross Youth Club at Aichi Shukutoku High School. The *origami* cranes, folded in many types of paper, were handed out, filling the hospital with a burst of color and hope. Confined to bed and with little to do, many of the patients were inspired to begin folding cranes themselves.

When Shigeo visited Sadako that night, she beamed with excitement as he walked in the door. "Look, Father!" she exclaimed. "*Origami* cranes!" Sadako loved the cranes but did not know their significance. "Why did they send us *origami* cranes, Father?" she wondered.

As Shigeo looked at the cranes, he told her, "Giving paper cranes to someone in the hospital means that you hope they'll get well soon."

"Why is that?" asked Sadako.

"There's an old story that if you fold a thousand paper cranes, your wish will come true," explained Shigeo. Sadako's eyes lit up.

Shigeo explained the legend to her. In Japan, he said, the crane is considered a mystical creature and, in folklore, is said to live for one thousand years. An ancient Japanese legend promises that anyone who folds one thousand cranes, one for each year of a crane's life, will be granted a wish. This story made cranes a favorite gift for anyone experiencing a life event, especially someone getting married or suffering from an illness.

After Shigeo left the hospital for the evening, Sadako told Kiyo she wanted to try folding some herself. With the legend in mind, she committed to folding a thousand cranes. She wanted her wish to come true. She wanted to be well, to return to school, and to live with her family again. Sadako pinned her hopes on the legend of the crane and poured her limited energy into folding.

Sadako pursued her new passion, day and night. Unlike today, paper was very costly in Japan in 1955. She limited her paper size to exactly 7.5 centimeters, the equivalent of about three square inches, and carefully cut each piece to her exacting standards. Sadako asked her many friends all over the hospital to find every scrap of paper they possibly could. The nurses gave Sadako the foil paper that shielded x-ray film during transport and the paper wrappings from medicine bottles. Other patients in the hospital saved candy wrappers and the colorful wrap from get-well gifts they received. Everyone pitched in and provided as much paper as they could for Sadako's pursuit. She slowly and delicately folded each paper as she received it and placed the cranes in empty candy boxes until they were overflowing. When she ran out of boxes, she filled her drawstring purse with the cranes, for safekeeping. Kiyo folded with her sometimes, and other visitors, patients, and nurses helped to fold when they could.

Sadako's purse, displayed at the Hiroshima Peace Memorial Museum

When her purse was full, Masahiro began to string the cranes on lines of thread for Sadako and hang them from the ceiling of her hospital room. Soon her room was filled with *origami* cranes, made from all sizes, colors, and types of paper. Shigeo said she would wear herself out if she kept up her pace. But Sadako was determined and told him she had a plan. If she folded a thousand cranes, she would get better. There was no stopping her. Her wish had to be granted. She had to get better.

With every day that passed, Sadako became more determined to realize her wish, folding her desire to live into each crane. The folding became a meditation, a focusing of her mind and energy. The number of cranes began to lose its importance. Each crane that was folded carried her dream. Her folding skills got better through practice. Each crane she folded was perfect and beautiful.

As the days passed and the number of cranes grew, Sadako's condition worsened. Her pain and discomfort increased. But to Sadako, this was only a signal she needed to fold faster and more often. She had to reach her goal. Then she would be healthy again.

› Chapter 18 ‹

Little Outings

Sadako's doctor was concerned with her deteriorating condition. She was not doing well. There was little that could be done for her now. Wanting her to enjoy what time she had left, the doctor decided to allow her to go home again for short visits when she felt up to it. The comfort of her family, and giving her as much of a normal life as possible, would be the best medicine now. Sadako wondered if folding the cranes brought this delightful gift of freedom from the confines of the hospital. She did not realize it was a signal that the doctor had given up hope.

Each August 6, the Hiroshima Peace Memorial Ceremony is held at the Peace Park in Hiroshima to console the souls of those who were lost due to the atomic bombing, as well as pray for the realization of everlasting world peace. Sadako received the doctor's permission to leave the hospital and attend with her family.

The night before the Peace Ceremony, Sadako arrived at her family's little shack in Moto-machi. Her body was wrapped in bandages, hiding the purple spots that were covering her skin. Masahiro and her two younger siblings were always happy to see her and were still mostly unaware of the pain Sadako was enduring.

"Do you want to go get some candy?" Sadako asked her younger brother and sister. The children were excited to go but soon realized Sadako was not doing well. Even they began to notice that Sadako struggled to walk and appeared to be in pain.

"Are you okay?" they asked their big sister. Sadako assured them she was fine. Fujiko waved to them as they headed to the store.

"I'm looking forward to tomorrow's ceremony!" Sadako shouted back to their mother as they headed for town. "Everyone will be there!"

The skies were clear the next morning as the family headed out for the Peace Ceremony. Everyone walked slowly so that Sadako could keep up. The sunny skies reminded Masahiro of the day the atomic bomb fell.

Sadako, shortly before the Hiroshima Peace Memorial Ceremony at Peace Park, August 6, 1955

Just before the ceremony began, Sadako felt weak and needed to rest. She sat under a tree, looking for relief from the hot August sun. Suddenly her gums started to bleed and wouldn't stop. "Mom... blood," she whispered.

When Fujiko looked at her, she saw her gums were bleeding and knew it was one of the symptoms of leukemia. Shigeo removed a handkerchief from his pocket to mop up the blood running from Sadako's mouth. But it just kept coming. Fujiko looked on in horror, knowing this was a sign of advanced atomic bomb disease. "Give me more tissue," requested

Shigeo. Soon, all the tissue was gone, and the bleeding continued. Sadako had to leave before the ceremony began.

On the train ride to the hospital, Sadako looked blankly at the sights of the city, blood staining her pale face. "Is it true that a white blood count over 100,000 means a person will die?" Sadako asked her father.

"That's silly, Sadako," he replied. "That's just a superstition." Sadako smiled weakly, accepting her father's reassuring words with stoic silence. But Sadako knew the truth.

Doctors at the Red Cross Hospital quickly treated Sadako when she arrived and sent her back home. But she was unable to attend the Peace Ceremony.

Sadako returned to the hospital on Monday, August 8, and began folding cranes with new vigor. When she finished fifty more cranes, Masahiro helped her string them together and hang them from the ceiling. Her hospital room twinkled with the tiny birds, fluttering overhead.

The roof became her sanctuary. When Masahiro came to visit, she invited him to go with her. "*Nī-chan*, the Milky Way is really beautiful. Let's go to the rooftop and see it!"

Little Outings

Masahiro had never been to the roof before and thought it sounded fun.

"Okay, let's go!" he replied.

> *Nī-chan* is Japanese for "older brother." *Nē-chan* means "older sister."

Sadako struggled to climb the stairs, dragging each foot and laboring with each step. Until that moment, Masahiro thought Sadako would soon be better and that their lives would return to normal. Seeing her condition now, however, he suddenly realized her fate. Masahiro took Sadako by the hand, easing her up the steps. Sadako was embarrassed but grateful for the help. Her hand felt small and feverish to Masahiro. He held on tight. No more teasing. No more horseplay. Masahiro suddenly realized Sadako was dying.

When they got to the rooftop, Sadako's eyes sparkled as she gazed at the night sky. "*Nī-chan*, look at the stars!" she exclaimed.

"Yeah, it sure is beautiful," replied Masahiro, feeling a heavy melancholy and enormous sense of wonder at the same time.

After a long while, Sadako was overcome with fatigue. "I need to rest now," she nearly whispered. Masahiro carefully guided Sadako down the stairs and safely back to her room.

Little Outings

Sadako returned to her bed, and Masahiro went home with a new appreciation of Sadako and deeper understanding of her condition.

Despite their financial troubles, Sadako's parents wanted to do everything they could for her when she was at home. Shigeo and Fujiko planned to close the barbershop during Japan's annual Obon Festival in the middle of August and take Sadako to the sea and on a tour of local attractions like the Hiroshima Children's Culture Hall. Sadako worried about so much money being spent on her. She told her father she was a bad child for causing so much expense. Shigeo and Fujiko were heartbroken. They worried they could not do enough for her with their limited resources. They only wanted the best for Sadako.

Sadako was concerned about her family's situation but still looked forward to her short break from the hospital. Many of her relatives had given money to Sadako when they visited her over the past many months. Instead of buying things for herself, Sadako saved the money. Shortly before the weekend, she went to the hospital gift shop and bought presents for her family. When she arrived home, she was carrying a handbag with a bell on it and a big *furoshiki*-wrapped bundle. "I bought matching *geta* for everyone," Sadako beamed, handing out the new sandals.

> *Geta* are traditional Japanese footwear. They are similar to flip-flops but made with a cloth strap and wooden sole.

Sadako never wasted money, so Masahiro and her parents were surprised by the gifts. "*Nē-chan*, thank you!" exclaimed her younger brother and sister. Sadako laughed when she saw the happiness her gifts brought to them. She felt so much better at home and loved her role of taking care of others.

But in the middle of this happy time, the loan sharks appeared in front of the house. Shigeo and Fujiko confronted them at the door. "Our daughter has just come home for a visit," they said. "Could you leave us alone today?" The loan sharks agreed and reluctantly disappeared. But Sadako was listening and was reminded again about the family's financial troubles.

Next door to the Sasakis lived the Ishikawa family. They too had been exposed to the atomic bomb and had suffered. The Ishikawa and Sasaki families had become good friends, and Mrs. Ishikawa always doted on Sadako. When Sadako saw the loan sharks at their door, she

Little Outings

went next door to the Ishikawa's house. "Have the debt collectors been coming by a lot?" she asked. Sadako was worried about what was going on at her house. She was also worried that the loan sharks were bothering the Ishikawa family as well as her own.

"Sadako, everything is okay," Mrs. Ishikawa said. "Don't pay any attention to them. Just concentrate on getting well. Your mother and father are working hard, so you need to work hard, too." Mrs. Ishikawa spoke from the heart, and with a cheerful, soothing voice. Sadako lifted her head and smiled in agreement.

During Sadako's visit home, Shigeo and Fujiko noticed that she was losing weight and looking pale. They worried she was spending too much energy folding cranes. But they couldn't stop her from doing something that brought her so much happiness and hope. The crane folding made her think of the future and gave her a goal. When Sadako returned to the hospital at the end of the weekend, she continued to fold more cranes.

On August 19, Sadako attended an event for Chinese delegates visiting the hospital. A new song, *Genbaku-o-Yurusumaji* was sung. The lyrics moved Sadako deeply. After the event, she and

Kiyo went to the roof. They tried to remember every word. The two girls gazed out over the city and sang as loudly as their weakened bodies could manage.

Genbaku-o-Yurusumaji

Our hometown was burned down.
We buried the charred remains of the ones we loved.
White flowers are now in bloom.
We must never allow a third atomic bombing.
We must never allow a third atomic bombing of our homeland.
The sea was stormy.
Black rain fell.
No days of joy.
Fishing boats were idle.
We must never allow a third atomic bombing.
We must never allow a third atomic bombing in the sea of our homeland.
The sky of our homeland hung heavily above us.
The black cloud covered the land that day, too.
There was no sunlight in the sky.
We must never allow a third atomic bombing.
We must never allow a third atomic bombing in the sky of our homeland.
People in the same motherland,
Labored hard to build their wealth and happiness.
Now, everything has disappeared.
We must never allow a third atomic bombing.
We must never allow a third atomic bombing in the world.

› Chapter 19 ‹

A Secret Wish

Toward the end of August, Sadako had completed folding a thousand cranes. She was happy she had reached her goal, but she felt no better. In fact, she was so weak that she barely celebrated her accomplishment of folding so many cranes. Her wish had not come true.

Kiyo felt terrible for Sadako. She knew how hard Sadako had worked to fold the thousand cranes. She could see that Sadako was feeling no better for all her efforts. To make matters worse for Sadako, Kiyo was pronounced cured of tuberculosis and was being released from the hospital. Sadako was happy for Kiyo but knew she would soon be alone in the room she had shared with her friend for so many months. Sadako put on her bravest face. She assured Kiyo not to worry. She would just fold another thousand cranes, and try again.

By early September, Sadako was too weak to go to the nurses' station, the rooftop, or much of anywhere else. She spent her days in bed, using what little energy she had to fold cranes. Each crane now took longer. Lying flat on her back as she folded, Sadako often needed to rest between folds. But, slowly the number of finished cranes increased.

Without her friend Kiyo to help collect paper, her supply began to dwindle. Sadako was forced to use smaller and smaller scraps. Some cranes she folded were not much bigger than a grain of rice. She used a needle from a sewing kit to guide the tiny and intricate folds, making sure each crease was precise.

Since Kiyo's release from the hospital, Sadako felt more alone than ever before. As her condition worsened, her parents tried to be with her as much as possible, doing their best to fill her lonely hours.

Shigeo arrived one evening after work with a terrible headache. His days were long, and he was carrying many burdens. But Shigeo wanted to be there for Sadako as much as possible. Sitting at her bedside, he soon fell fast asleep. Despite her failing body, her difficulty walking, and the pain each step caused, Sadako sneaked away to the

A Secret Wish

pharmacy while he slept. When he awoke, Sadako was folding cranes in bed. She smiled at him and handed him some aspirin. "Here, Papa, take this," she said. Even in her enormous suffering, she found the strength to care for others. Shigeo smiled with pride and melancholy to know he had such a remarkable daughter. Her compassion made him forget all about his headache.

Seeing Sadako struggle now with even the simplest movements during his next visit, Shigeo expressed his concern. "I wish you would not fold so many cranes," he told her. "I worry it is taking too much of your strength."

"But, Papa, I must!" she replied. "I have a new wish. It's a secret! You'll see when it comes true." Shigeo said no more. He knew he could not take away something that brought her such happiness and filled her with hope.

One night, Sadako began to worry about how much time her mother was spending at the hospital. She knew her two brothers and sister needed her also. She encouraged her mother to go home and assured her that she would be okay. But, as she spoke, tears began to well up in her eyes. It was the only time throughout her illness that Fujiko saw Sadako cry. Fujiko knew she must stay with her more often. She started spending every night in the room with her.

"I wonder how many years it's been since I've been able to sleep in the same room with you," Sadako asked her mother. "I'm so happy!" She was in high spirits, happy to have this short time with her mother. Even though Sadako had a premonition about her own death, she pretended she would soon be well, so as not to worry her mother.

"Sadako, let me comb your hair," Fujiko offered one night. Sadako's mother loosened her long braid and picked up a comb.

"Sadako, what's this secret you told Papa you had?" Sadako's mother asked as she combed her hair.

"Secret?" Sadako's eyes twinkled.

"Papa is really curious," Sadako's mother said. "He told me that you were thinking about something, and then he asked you what it was."

"Oh! That secret!" Sadako giggled.

Fujiko finished combing Sadako's hair and turned her around. Sadako leaned in and whispered in her mother's ear. "If you can keep a secret from Papa, I'll tell you." Her mother nodded, and Sadako smiled. "The cranes I'm

A Secret Wish

folding now, I'm praying that Papa's debt will be repaid soon. But if you tell him, he'll worry about it. Please keep the secret!"

Sadako's mother was overwhelmed with emotion. "Sadako, thank you! I raised such a thoughtful child. I don't think I've ever been this happy." She hugged Sadako as tears rolled down her cheeks.

The next morning, when Fujiko returned to the barbershop to work and tend to the three other children during the day, Sadako continued to fold cranes. Masahiro visited often, helping to string and hang them as tiny beacons of hope above Sadako's hospital bed.

As Sadako's illness progressed, the purple spots she had seen on Yuki's skin began to appear on every part of her own body. The skin lesion covered her entire abdomen. Her hair started to fall out in clumps. Sadako surely understood her condition and fate. And yet, she continued to fold cranes, centering her mind and focusing on perfecting her technique. Each crane took painful and intense effort as she folded. Sadako continued to fold until finally, she could fold no more. Sadako had folded more than thirteen hundred cranes.

› Chapter 20 ‹

Pain-Free at Last

By early October, her condition had worsened dramatically. Sadako went home for a brief visit on October 1, but returned to the hospital on October 3. Her gums were bleeding, and her muscles ached. She suffered from high fevers and swelling, and the purple spots continued to grow in number. Walking was difficult, and soon breathing was too. Fujiko arrived every day after work and continued to spend every night with Sadako. The family visited her often, hoping to boost her spirits and take her mind off her pain.

But Sadako could no longer get out of bed. Her left leg had turned a deep purple and was swollen and painful. She could not sleep. The doctor tried to make her comfortable and gave her a blood transfusion on October 24. But Sadako refused any medications to reduce her pain. She said she did not want to endure the side effects of the medicine. But her family feared she was only concerned with the high cost of the drugs and did not want to burden them with any more expenses.

At eight o'clock in the morning on October 25, the doctor examined Sadako. He told her mother that Sadako had only a few hours to live. Fujiko called Shigeo on the telephone. "Sadako is... Sadako is..." She couldn't get the words out. Shigeo understood: Sadako's time was near. He called the schools and requested that his two older children meet him at Sadako's bedside, then he bundled little Eiji in a basket on his bicycle and pedaled as fast as he could to reach the hospital in time. When Masahiro and Mitsue got the message at school, they immediately made their way to the hospital. After letting Sadako's classmates know about her condition, Mr. Nomura rushed to Sadako's bedside as well. As soon as Sadako's classmates heard the news, they were all determined to be with her too, united again, hearts beating as one, just like their days on the track. Soon, Sadako's hospital room was overflowing with family and friends, wishing her well and lending their support.

Pain-Free at Last

At last, in Sadako's final moments, Shigeo insisted that the doctor administer morphine, giving Sadako relief from the intense pain that wracked her body. A peaceful expression overcame her as her mother held her hand and wept at her bedside.

"I'm okay, Mom," Sadako whispered. "Don't cry." Suddenly Sadako noticed that her room had filled up with family and friends. "Why is everyone here?" she asked. Her father urged her to eat something. Sadako requested tea on rice, a traditional Japanese comfort food. But the hospital cafeteria in the basement was closed. Shigeo asked Masahiro to run a local restaurant to buy the treat. Sadako, lingering near death, was still looking out for her family. "The Red Cross Hospital rice is fine," she whispered, knowing that buying it from a restaurant would be more expensive. But Masahiro ran to a local restaurant and returned with the rice. Shigeo blocked Sadako's view of Masahiro as he carefully put the rice into a Red Cross Hospital bowl and poured the tea over the top. Shigeo checked the temperature of the tea with his lips, then fed a small mouthful to Sadako. "This tastes good," Sadako said. She ate one more bite. "Father, mother, everyone, thank you," she whispered. She looked at each visitor, one by one. Then her eyes gently closed. Moments later, as if drifting off to sleep, Sadako passed away.

Sadako's thousand paper cranes danced above as her family wept in grief.

The Children's Peace Monument at Hiroshima's Peace Park, with a figure of Sadako at the top of the statue

> Chapter 21 ‹

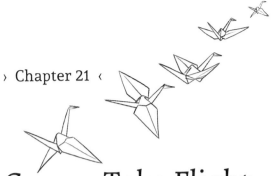

Cranes Take Flight

*A*fter Sadako's passing, her nurses found the small paper tucked under the mattress in her hospital room. Carefully written dates and numbers marked Sadako's blood cell count over the past many months. Since discovering her chart at the nurses' station that day, Sadako had been recording her blood count numbers and saving them in secret, tucked securely under her mattress. The family was shocked when they learned about her record keeping and now knew that Sadako understood her fate all along. Shigeo gripped Sadako's scratch paper in his hand. Recollections of Sadako welled up inside of him as tears streamed down his cheeks.

Not only had Sadako overcome her fear of death, but she also poured her love for her family into her every thought and action. Even when she was hurting, suffering, and scared, and knew she was close to death, Sadako always put on a happy face in front of her family. Every crane she folded became a wish of happiness for them.

The day after her passing, a small notice appeared in the Hiroshima newspaper.

> "Sadako Sasaki, student at Nobori-chō Junior High School, had been sick since last fall with the atomic bomb disease. She was exposed to the atomic bomb ten years ago, and now she is gone. Seventh-grader. Age twelve."

Sadako's funeral was held at Shinkōji Temple, across the river from the Sasaki's home. It was a modest send-off, but the finest her family could afford. With money borrowed and donated, Shigeo arranged for sixteen taxis to bring Sadako's many friends, schoolmates, neighbors, and family to see her off for the final time.

Sadako was cremated in her dress-up *kimono*, accompanied by one of the wooden dolls her classmates had given her. She was surrounded by hundreds of the cranes she folded in her lifetime, and many more folded by her classmates. Shigeo and Fujiko told the mourners gathered at Sadako's funeral that they hoped the cranes would take Sadako to heaven, where she could watch over Hiroshima.

Other cranes Sadako had folded were given to her friends and classmates. The cranes became a reminder of Sadako and all those that suffered from the effects of war.

In the weeks that followed, Sadako's classmates, along with Mr. Nomura, talked about how best to remember Sadako. One of the girls suggested placing a marker in Hiroshima's Peace Park to remember her and all the other victims of *pika*. But without the money to create it, the children agreed that bringing flowers to her grave each month would have to do.

Soon after Sadako's death, Shigeo and Fujiko hosted a memorial for family and those closest to Sadako. Mr. Nomura was there, along with Ichirō Kawamoto, a young man who dedicated much of his time and money to help those most impacted by the bomb. Mr. Kawamoto had an idea, and he was eager to share it with those in attendance.

"I propose that we build a memorial statue for Sadako and all the children that died from the atomic bomb disease," he told them. "Together, we can make this dream a reality." Everyone who was there agreed to help.

Mr. Kawamoto proposed to Mr. Nomura that Sadako's classmates write a letter to distribute at the annual Principal's Convention, to be held soon in Hiroshima.

The students spent the next several days writing and designing their idea. They pooled their pocket money to buy the paper and borrowed the school's mimeograph machine to print two thousand flyers to distribute.

> ### LET'S BUILD A STATUE FOR THE CHILDREN OF THE ATOMIC BOMB
>
> We learned that school principals from all over Japan would be holding their meeting, and therefore we wish to share with you the following story:
>
> Our dear friend, Sadako Sasaki, died on October 25th. Since early childhood, she was our closest friend. We studied and played together. But in January of this year, the innocent Sadako suddenly became sick. After nine long months in the hospital, she died.

> Knowing that Sadako was aware of her fatal condition has made us very sad. But there is nothing we can do about it now. We do not want her death to have been in vain, so we hope to build a statue for all the children who died of the Atomic Bomb Disease. We are here today to make our project known to you honorable principals and to ask you to convey our message to all our fellow junior high school students throughout the country, and encourage them to support us. We came today to make this plea.
>
> *Hiroshima Municipal Nobori-chō*
> *Junior High School Seventh Graders*
> *All the Classmates of the late Sadako Sasaki*

"Please read this!" the students shouted as they stood outside the Principal's Convention. One by one the two thousand flyers were distributed. Many of the principals were encouraging; some even gave donations to the students for their statue. Sadako's classmates were bolstered by their success and vowed to fight even harder to make the monument a reality.

In the coming months, many principals read the flyer to their students. Soon students all over Japan embraced the idea of a statue and began fundraising campaigns of their own.

By December, more than 432,000 *yen* ($1200 American dollars) had been raised.

Sadako's classmates formed a group called *Kokeshi-no-kai*, named after the *kokeshi* doll that Sadako kept at her bedside in the hospital. The students became effective fundraisers in Hiroshima and started the formation of the Hiroshima Children and Students' Council for the Creation of Peace, which included students from all the schools, as well as Masahiro and Kiyo.

Soon, schools across the nation were engaged, and contributions quickly reached 5,400,000 *yen* ($15,000 American dollars). Their impossible dream had come true.

The statue of Sadako, named *Genbaku no Ko no Zō* (The Statue for the Children of the Atomic Bomb) was unveiled in the Peace Memorial Park in Hiroshima on May 5, 1958. Engraved on its base is the following:

> *This is our Cry*
> *This is our Prayer*
> *To Create Peace in the World*

Hiroshima was once again a beautiful city. Black rain no longer fell from the skies, only rays of sunshine. The war was receding into the

Cranes Take Flight

distance. But Sadako, and hundreds of thousands of others, innocent victims of the war, were gone.

Eventually, Sadako's final wish did come true. Her family, at last, worked their way out of debt. Her three siblings grew up without falling victim to the atomic bomb disease that took Sadako's life, and they went on to live productive and rewarding lives. Happiness slowly returned to the family, with Sadako always in their hearts and minds.

And while she was not cured of her illness, Sadako lives on in the thousands of paper cranes that are folded around the world every day in her memory, and in memory of all those lost to the tragedy of war.

Masahiro and Sadako behind their home, March 1949

Epilogue

A note from Masahiro Sasaki

It's been more than sixty years since Sadako died. I was a junior high school student then, and I had a lot of feelings I couldn't sort out at the time. But now I can understand the things that I learned from Sadako during her short life and the things that she hid in her heart.

In her brief twelve years, Sadako loved her family, and we loved her. Our parents showed compassion for Sadako during her illness, and Sadako showed compassion toward our parents during their financial difficulties. Sadako taught us the importance of "*omoiyari-no-kokoro*," the showing consideration for others, no matter life's circumstances.

In Japanese culture, *omoiyari-no-kokoro*, the act of showing empathy and concern, is taught from an early age and considered one of the most important things a child can learn in preschool.

Sadako folded her prayers into the origami cranes which she so earnestly made. The first thousand cranes were an ardent prayer that she would be cured of her illness. With the next thousand cranes, she prayed for our father's debt to be resolved. Our family prayed for Sadako's happiness. And Sadako, despite her illness, folded for ours. She folded so that she could go home, and for her family's happiness.

What I learned from Sadako was that from a heart that values love and compassion, we can be in perfect empathy with one another, respecting and understanding one another deeply. Even when her leukemia worsened and her legs hurt so much that she couldn't walk, Sadako still treated her family with compassion, thinking that if her family knew of her hardship, they would worry about her. So for those of us who have no worries, there's no reason for us not to treat those around us with compassion.

When Sadako was in the hospital, not once did she say, "It hurts," "I'm in pain," or "Help me." Not once did she speak with bitterness or hatred toward the atomic bomb or the country that dropped it on Hiroshima. I am also a *hibakusha*, but Sadako taught me to "forget" the name of the country which dropped the atomic bomb.

More than seventy years have passed since the war ended. There is no point in discussing

Epilogue

whether the use of atomic bombs was right or not. The issue is what kind of ordeal the people of the world had to go through due to war. This should never be forgotten by any of the countries that participated. We need to teach our children the lesson that any war should not happen. The hearts of resentment and retaliation that can emerge from unforgettable experiences of the past should never be handed over to children who will hold the future in their hands. We must throw away our resentment. From hatred, only hatred and hearts of revenge will be born.

To move forward, we must unite with others. The wisest choice is to recognize and respect the differences in our ways of thinking, creating a new stage of hope that includes open discussions amongst all people. To overcome certain naturally existing differences between us, we should have a generous mind, accepting each other. This is the first step we should make and is the essence of *omoiyari-no-kokoro*. It is important to always keep it in our minds. Extending consideration and compassion to others is a security code that can open the doors of the hearts of all people living on this Earth.

Pure eyes of children, eyes seeking something, hearts of believing anything, we do not defile them with our egoism.

Sadako died when she was twelve. I imagine she wanted to play more, study more, talk with her friends more, eat more… There were lots of things she wanted to do. But her life ended before she had a chance to experience those things. Sadako was regretful because she didn't have the opportunity to do them. Therefore, we should think about the incredible value our uneventful daily lives have. We should be thankful for walking, eating, playing, studying, the ordinary things we spend time doing every day.

Before her death, Sadako was aware that she had leukemia. That was why she became more and more compassionate toward our parents, as she did not want them to be sad and concerned about her.

In your daily life, you will face many problems and experience much happiness. And I suppose you will laugh a lot and shed a lot of tears. But you'll also study a lot, and talk with your friends a lot. Do you think you are compassionate and caring to your friends? Do you practice *omoiyari-no-kokoro*?

Cry when you need to if you have a lot of troubles, but grow up with a kind heart, filled with compassion. When you are able to behave in that way, I am sure you will notice that you have changed. This is the way to create a small bit of peace in your surroundings. When we can connect such small bits of peace together, we will surely have greater hope of peace in the future. This proves that you are living your life to its fullest.

Sadako's cranes, displayed at the Peace Museum, Hiroshima

A note from Sue DiCicco

Over time, Sadako's story spread. She touched the hearts of people everywhere and transformed the *origami* crane into an international symbol of peace and hope. Individuals and groups in every corner on earth have been moved to create their own events and remembrances to honor the brave young girl who believed in the power of her dream.

In December 2012, I myself began a journey that unexpectedly tied my life to Sadako and her dream. Like everyone else in America, I was stunned and horrified to hear of the Sandy Hook Elementary School shootings in Connecticut. Mass shootings had become commonplace in America. Each time, the country became enraged. Each time, our politicians and everyday citizens engaged in loud and polarizing debates, looking for answers. Each time, no solutions were offered. No changes were made. No plan was enacted. This particular shooting seemed especially heinous. Twenty children, six and seven years old, were gunned down, along with six of their teachers, and the shooter's own mother. The horrific nature of the crime prompted me to believe we could no longer wait for our politicians to find solutions. I began to wonder what each of us could do to stem the tide of violence that was sweeping our world.

I have spent my life working as an artist, first as an animator at Disney, and later, as an illustrator of children's books. My experience in those fields led me to feel confident that I knew how to engage people, especially children, in a fun way. How could I translate that into an actionable plan, something that could unite people and create more understanding?

I posted my thoughts on Facebook. Soon, an active dialogue began. Among the participants was my longtime friend Deborah Moldow.

Epilogue

Deborah also happened to be a co-chair of the International Day of Peace NGO Committee at the United Nations. "Why don't you create a project for Peace Day?" she asked.

For several days, I retreated to my studio and began to explore possibilities. How could I share my love of art with children, while at the same time bring them all together in a vision of peace and understanding?

I set my mind to creating a global, inclusive art event, something everyone, everywhere could do. This limited my choices. No special brushes, scissors, or paints could be required. Many groups around the world may not have access to those. The project needed to be universal in its appeal, and something that could be easily shared with others.

I learned to fold *origami* as a child and always had a love for Japan, its culture, and elegant aesthetic. I had never heard Sadako's story. But I knew of the *origami* crane and that it was a symbol of peace for many in the world. What if I invited every child in the world to fold a crane, write a message of peace on its wings, and then offer a way for them to trade it with another child somewhere in the world?

With the power and potential of the Internet and my friends involved in the United Nations International Day of Peace behind me, I launched my idea, now called The Peace Crane Project, shortly before Peace Day in 2013. My friend and videographer Rubia Braun stepped in to make a series of videos for our launch. Quickly, classroom and community groups around the world began to sign up, taking the project in directions I could never have dreamed, connecting in ways beyond my wildest hopes.

I soon discovered that many students participating in The Peace Crane Project knew the story of Sadako. August 6 had been declared Sadako Day in my hometown of Santa Barbara, California, in 1996. Many children learn her story each year and take the time to commemorate her life and all those lost in the horrors of war. Several teachers asked if I could arrange peace crane exchanges for them on this special day as well. By 2014, the Peace Crane Project was hosting many thousands of exchanges in August for Sadako Day and again in September for the UN Peace Day.

Teachers and community leaders soon found they could make the Peace Crane Project part of their curriculum and activities all year long.

Epilogue

In 2015, the Peace Crane Project began hosting exchanges every day of the year.

Today, as I type this in May 2018, more than two million children have participated, meeting other students, learning geography, practicing their writing, strengthening their hand-eye coordination, and building an appreciation for all the people and cultures of the world.

If you would like to join the Peace Crane Project to trade cranes and greetings of peace with other students all around the planet or offer your support, please visit my website: *PeaceCraneProject.org*.

My ultimate hope is that, regardless of your success in folding a crane, you will remember Sadako and keep a vision of peace in your thoughts and actions. Together, peace is possible. If we believe, we will succeed.

How to Fold an Origami Peace Crane

To fold a crane you will need a single sheet of paper.

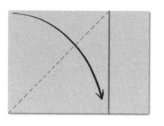

1. Fold your paper in half, diagonally. If your paper is not square, cut along the solid line.

2. Fold in half again.

3. Bring top point of top layer down to meet bottom point, opening paper as you go, to form a square.

4. Does your paper look like this? If so, turn it over. If no, go back to step 3.

5. Repeat fold on this side.

6. Fold sides of top layer to middle, then unfold.

7. Fold top down to side creases, then lift top layer upward.

8. Create a boat-like shape by folding sides inward.

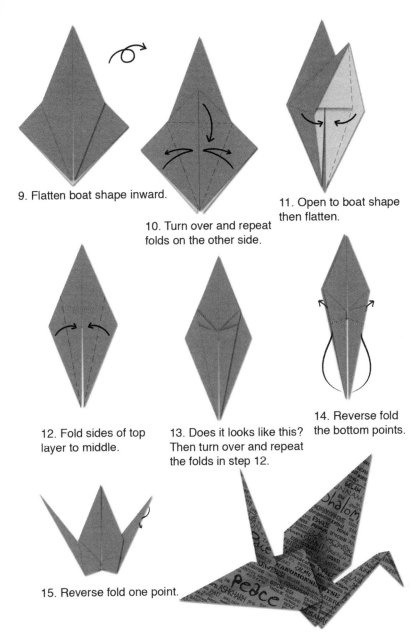

ABOUT THE AUTHORS

Masahiro Sasaki, Sadako's older brother, was born in Hiroshima in 1941. Masahiro, along with Sadako, were exposed to the atomic bombing in 1945. As a teenager, he joined the Acting Construction Committee to build The Children's Monument of the Atomic Bomb, completed in 1958.

Since 2000, Masahiro has dedicated himself to sharing Sadako's true story, and the plight of all atomic war survivors with the world. Masahiro received the Hiroshima Citizen's Award in 2007 and was awarded the Spirit of America Award from the National Council for the Social Studies, the first non-American to receive it. He established *The Sadako Legacy*, a nonprofit organization, in 2009. To inspire others, he has donated Sadako's cranes to venues all around the world.

Today, Masahiro gives lectures globally and promotes activities to connect people for peace

He lives in Fukuoka, Japan.

Sue DiCicco began her career as a Disney animator, one of the first women to achieve that position. In addition to her work as an animator, Sue is a sculptor and prolific author/illustrator of books for children, including *Origami Peace Cranes: Friendships Take Flight*, a story designed to encourage connection and friendship through *origami* cranes. An early pioneer of the Internet, Sue designed and created the world's first online schoolhouse, serving up to 300,000 school children per event in the 1990s.

Propelled by a desire to creatively connect students from every corner of the world in a vision of peace, Sue founded the Peace Crane Project in 2012.

In addition to hosting the Peace Crane Project, Sue now speaks at venues globally, inviting listeners to explore and embrace the power and the potential of the Internet to connect students in creating a more understanding, educated, integrated, and peaceful future.

She lives in Santa Barbara, California.

"Books to Span the East and West"

Tuttle Publishing was founded in 1832 in the small New England town of Rutland, Vermont [USA]. Our core values remain as strong today as they were then—to publish best-in-class books which bring people together one page at a time. In 1948, we established a publishing outpost in Japan—and Tuttle is now a leader in publishing English-language books about the arts, languages and cultures of Asia. The world has become a much smaller place today and Asia's economic and cultural influence has grown. Yet the need for meaningful dialogue and information about this diverse region has never been greater. Over the past seven decades, Tuttle has published thousands of books on subjects ranging from martial arts and paper crafts to language learning and literature—and our talented authors, illustrators, designers and photographers have won many prestigious awards. We welcome you to explore the wealth of information available on Asia at **www.tuttlepublishing.com**.